The Easy Art of Cooking with Nuts

D1601288

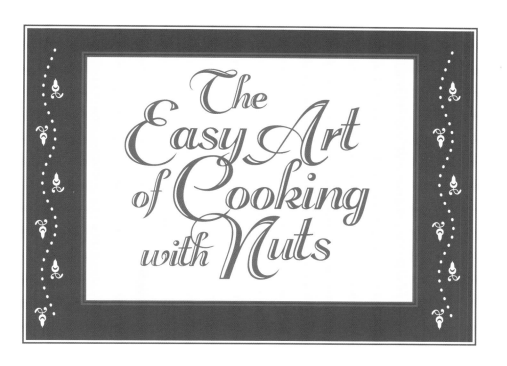

The Easy Art of Cooking with Nuts

by *Christin Fjeld Drake*
Photographs by Gene Balzer

NORTHLAND PUBLISHING

First Edition

ISBN 0-87358-583-6
Library of Congress Catalog Card Number 94-11134
Library of Congress Cataloging-in-Publication Data
Drake, Christin.
        The easy art of cooking with nuts / by Christin Drake ;
        photographs by Gene Balzer. — 1st ed.
            p.   cm.
        Includes index.
        ISBN 0-87358-583-6 : $12.95
        I. Cookery (Nuts) I. Title
    TX814.D73 1994
    641.6'45—dc20
    94-11134

Manufactured in Hong Kong by Wing King Tong
Designed by Julie Sullivan
Edited by Jill Mason and Erin Murphy
Pictured on the cover: Chicken Breasts with
    Walnuts and Artichoke Hearts, page 59;
    and Hazelnut Cheesecake, page 85.
Pictured on the frontispiece: Apple Walnut pastries, page 7;
    Sunshine Coconut Cookies, page 80;
    Almond Apple Pie, page 66.
Food styling by Christin Fjeld Drake
Tableware and accessories provided by Dillard's Department Store,
the Emporium, and the Kitchen Source.

0480/5M/8-94

Special thanks to my friends
Karen Bannon and Linda Condert
for their valuable help.

And to my family and friends who were
made to indulge themselves in my nutty experiments.
I can only hope they enjoyed it.

Contents

Introduction

Nuts—what a wonderful gift from nature. They come individually wrapped and ready to eat. A nut's storage time is long and its contents are rich in amino acids, complex carbohydrates, protein, vitamins B and E, and magnesium. Each variety of nut has its own value, taste, and texture.

The English word *nut* comes from the Old English *hnutu*, and the Latin words *nux* and *nutrients*, meaning "to nourish." It is understandable that nuts have been an important food source since the Stone Age and remain a valuable and tasty addition to almost any food today.

In this book, I have used the most common nuts available: almonds, Brazil nuts, cashews, chestnuts, coconut, hazelnuts, macadamia nuts, peanuts (raw unless otherwise noted), pecans, pine (or piñon) nuts, pistachios, walnuts, and water chestnuts. These nuts can be found in health food stores, farmer's markets, and grocery stores.

When you buy nuts, they should seem heavy for their sizes and should be as fresh as possible, since the high fat content can turn them rancid. Unshelled last longer than shelled nuts (up to six months) and should be stored in a ventilated container, such as a paper bag, in a dark, cool place. Shelled nuts should be stored in an airtight container also in a dark, cool place. Shelf life for most shelled nuts is about six weeks. Shelled nuts can be frozen in order to prolong shelf life.

In the recipes that follow, the different nuts can be exchanged for one another, but the texture and flavor of each dish will change a bit as a result. It's all a matter of personal preference.

Cooking is not an exact science; even if we measure exactly and follow the instructions word for word, results will vary due to influences such as the barometric pressure, how many times the batter was stirred, how many times we peeked at the cake while it was baking, the sweetness of the fruit used, the age of the meat, the freshness of the vegetables, the flavor of the butter, the grind of the flour, the age of the eggs, and the temperature of the room.

Cooking is creative—it is an art. It gratifies all of our senses and satisfies our deepest instincts to eat good food and feed others. Experiment and don't worry about making mistakes. From mistakes comes experience, and experience makes a great cook.

Enjoy!

Tips

SHELLING

• To shell almonds, cashews, walnuts, Brazil nuts, hazelnuts, macadamia nuts and pecans: Use a nutcracker or hammer.
• To shell peanuts and pistachios: Break shells open with your hands.
• To shell piñon nuts: Roast for 10 minutes, then, using a flat stone or coffee cup, grind them. Remove the kernels.

BLANCHING

Blanching is a method of preparation often used for almonds and pistachios. Bring a pot of water to boil. Drop the nuts in the water for 3 minutes or until the skins blister. Then, using a slotted spoon, remove the nuts from the water and rub them in a towel to remove the skins.

TOASTING

To toast nuts, heat the oven to 350° F. Spread nuts on a baking sheet and place in the oven. Bake for about 12 minutes, turning the nuts a few times. Or, toast the nuts in a heavy unoiled skillet for about 4 minutes, stirring constantly until they are light brown.

GRINDING

To grint nuts, use a nut grinder (best) or a food processor. Grind only a cup of nuts at a time, so that you don't overdo it and release the oil.

Breads and Breakfast Dishes

Almond Apple Muffins

1 cup plain yogurt
2 sticks butter, softened
4 eggs, beaten
4 cups flour
1 cup sugar
4 teaspoons baking powder
2 teaspoons cinnamon
3 cups apples, peeled, cut into
　　small chunks (chunky applesauce
　　can be substituted)
1 cup raisins
1 cup almonds, chopped fine
4 tablespoons coarse sugar

Preheat oven to 375° F. In a bowl, mix the yogurt, butter, and eggs. Stir in the flour, 1 cup sugar, baking powder, and cinnamon. Gently stir in the apples, raisins, and nuts. Spoon the batter into greased muffin tins, then sprinkle the 4 tablespoons coarse sugar on top. Bake for 20 minutes. Makes 32 muffins.

Almond Blintzes with Raspberries

BATTER
2 cups flour
½ cup almonds, ground
2 cups milk
1 teaspoon almond extract
5 eggs

RASPBERRY FILLING
3 cups cottage cheese
½ cup powdered sugar
1 cup raspberries (if frozen
　　berries are used, defrost and
　　drain before measuring)

TOPPING
4 tablespoons butter, melted
1 cup slivered almonds

Preheat oven to 400° F.
　　Combine all batter ingredients and beat until smooth and lump free.
　　Then combine all filling ingredients in a separate bowl, stir well, and set aside.
　　Make thin pancakes with the batter and fry on one side only. Fill each pancake with 2 tablespoons of filling, then fold into a package. Place the packages in a lightly greased ovenproof dish. Sprinkle with the melted butter and slivered almonds. Bake for 15 minutes. Serve with powdered sugar and fruit. Makes 12 blintzes.

Shown previous page:
Poppy Seed Pecan Muffins, page 5.

Almond December Buns

These buns taste particularly good warm.

BUNS
1 ½ cups milk
2 packages yeast
2 eggs
½ cup butter, melted and slightly cooled
½ cup sugar
5 ½ cups flour
½ teaspoon cardamom
½ teaspoon cinnamon
¾ cup almonds, blanched and ground
1 cup raisins
1 tablespoon grated lemon peel

GLAZE
1 egg white
4 teaspoons coarse sugar

Heat the milk until lukewarm. Dissolve the yeast in the milk; add the eggs and the melted butter and, using a fork, beat together. In a large bowl, combine the sugar, flour, spices, ground almonds, raisins, and lemon peel. Add the yeast mixture to the middle of the flour mixture and stir together. Knead the dough for 5 minutes on a lightly floured board and place it back in the bowl. Cover the bowl with a tea towel and set it in a cozy place. Let the dough rise for 1 ½ hours or until it has doubled in size.

Punch the dough down and knead it again for 5 minutes. Then pinch the dough into golf-ball–sized pieces and place them on a cookie tray. Brush each bun with the beaten egg white and sprinkle with coarse sugar. Again cover with a tea towel and set in a cozy place to rise for another 1 ½ hours.

Preheat oven to 350° F. and bake for 20 minutes or until golden brown. Makes 42 buns.

Almonds

Almonds have been cultivated in the Mediterranean and Asia for thousands of years and are presently grown commercially in Australia, the Canary Islands, Africa, and the southwestern U. S., including California.

The almond tree is from the same family as the peach, plum, and cherry trees. There are many different varieties of almond trees, but only two types of almonds: bitter and sweet. Bitter almond oils are used to make flavoring extracts and cosmetics. The sweet almond is the nut most frequently used in foods.

The almond grows in a shell that splits open easily when the nut is mature. The nut itself is protected by a thin, brown skin that can be removed by blanching, although almonds are also used unblanched. Almonds are high in protein, minerals, calories, and amino acids, and also contain vitamins B1, B2, B6, and E.

Nutty Granola

3 cups old-fashioned oats
1 ½ cups hazelnuts
½ cup honey
¼ cup vegetable oil
1 ½ teaspoons vanilla
1 ½ teaspoons cinnamon
½ cup dried apples, chopped
½ cup dried prunes, chopped
½ cup dried figs, chopped
½ cup dried apricots, chopped
½ cup raisins
¼ cup sesame seeds

Preheat oven to 350° F. Place the oats and hazelnuts on a lightly greased baking sheet and bake for 10 minutes. Warm the honey in a hot water bath until it is runny. Stir the oil, vanilla, and cinnamon into the honey; add the rest of the ingredients and mix. Add this mixture to the oats and hazelnuts and blend. Place the baking sheet in the oven for another 15–20 minutes. Remove from the oven and let the mixture cool. Store in an airtight container. Makes 12 cups of granola.

Hazelnut Pancakes with Strawberry Jam

These are not thick flapjacks but thin pancakes similar to crepes.

PANCAKES
3 cups flour
¾ cup hazelnuts, ground
6 tablespoons sugar
1 teaspoon vanilla
4 eggs
3 cups milk

STRAWBERRY JAM
4 cups strawberries, cleaned and hulled
1 cup sugar
1 tablespoon lemon juice
4 tablespoons water

In a bowl, blend the flour, hazelnuts, and sugar. Beat in the vanilla, eggs, and milk until the batter is smooth. Let the batter sit for 20 minutes while you make the strawberry jam.

Cut the big strawberries in half; leave the small ones as they are. Place the strawberries in a pot, add the sugar, lemon juice, and water, and bring to a boil. On low heat, simmer for 10 minutes.

Fry the pancakes in a hot skillet with a little oil or butter; the batter should just coat the bottom of the skillet. The pancakes should be light brown on both sides when done. Fold each pancake twice. Keep them warm until you are ready to eat. Top with jam before serving. Makes 20 pancakes.

Old-Fashioned Hazelnut Bread

1 ¾ cups warm milk
1 teaspoon sugar
2 packages yeast
3 tablespoons butter, melted
2 ¼ cups all-purpose flour
2 cups whole wheat flour
½ cup rye flour
1 ½ teaspoons salt
¾ cup hazelnuts, toasted
    and chopped fine
1 egg white

Pour the finger-warm milk into a bowl. Add the sugar and yeast, and stir until the yeast dissolves (about 5 minutes). Add the melted butter.

   In another large bowl, combine the flours, salt, and nuts, reserving 3 teaspoons of nuts. Add the yeast mixture and blend. Knead until the dough is smooth and elastic. Add more flour if the dough is sticky. Cover the dough with a tea towel and set it in a warm place to rise. In about 2 hours, the dough should be doubled in size. Take the dough out, punch it down, and knead it some more on a lightly floured board. Form the dough into a loaf and place it on a lightly greased cookie tray. Then allow it to rise once again to double in size.

   Preheat oven to 350° F. and bake for about 1 hour. Makes one loaf.

Apricot Pecan Spread

1 cup dried apricots
1 tablespoon honey
8 ounces cream cheese,
    at room temperature
½ cup pecans, chopped fine

Place the apricots in a bowl and cover them with hot water. Let them soak for 1 hour. Then drain them and place them in a food processor or blender. Add the remaining ingredients and blend well. Chill for 2 hours before using. Makes 2 cups of spread.

Poppy Seed Pecan Muffins

1 cup sugar
¼ cup butter
1 teaspoon grated orange peel
2 eggs
1 cup sour cream
1 cup whole wheat flour
1 cup all-purpose flour
2 ½ teaspoons baking powder
½ teaspoon salt
¼ teaspoon nutmeg
½ cup pecans, chopped
4 tablespoons poppy seeds

Preheat oven to 375° F. Beat the sugar and butter together. Add the orange peel, eggs, and sour cream. Stir in all dry ingredients; mix well. Pour the batter into muffin tins lined with cupcake papers. Bake for 20 minutes or until spongy on top. Makes 24 muffins.

Blueberry Walnut Muffins

2 sticks butter, soft
2 cups sugar
5 eggs
2 teaspoons vanilla
1 ½ cups sour cream
3 teaspoons baking powder
4 cups flour
½ cup wheat germ
4 cups blueberries, fresh or frozen
1 ½ cups walnuts, chopped fine

Preheat oven to 375° F. In a bowl, beat the butter and sugar until fluffy and white. Add the eggs, one at a time, and beat well. Add the vanilla and sour cream. Mix the dry ingredients together and stir into the egg batter. Fold in the blueberries and walnuts. Grease and flour muffin tins or line with paper baking cups. Fill three-quarters full with batter; bake for 30 minutes. Makes 36 muffins.

Walnuts

Walnuts, a favorite of gods of ancient mythology, are native to southwestern Europe and central Asia. They are cultivated in Italy, Germany, France, and California. The French for walnut is *la noix*, which also means simply "the nut." We have added *wal*, from the Old English *wealh*, which means "foreign."

High in fats and proteins, the walnut is also rich in vitamin C when green.

In France, walnut oil is used in salads. Walnuts are also used in syrups, cakes, breads, and stuffings. Walnut shells are used in glues and plastics.

Before using walnuts, make sure that the dark skin covering the nut is completely removed, or it will make food bitter.

Apple Walnut Pastries

PASTRY
1 cup warm milk
2 packages yeast
2 teaspoons sugar
2 eggs
6 cups flour
3 sticks butter, at room temperature

APPLE FILLING
6 apples, peeled and grated
½ cup sugar
½ cup raisins
½ cup walnuts, chopped
2 teaspoons lemon juice

GLAZE
1 cup powdered sugar
Several drops of lemon juice

In a bowl, mix the finger-warm milk with the yeast and sugar. When the yeast has dissolved, use a fork to beat in the eggs. In a large bowl, combine the flour with the yeast mixture and stir until well blended. Use your hands to quickly knead in the butter (the dough will be sticky). Cover the bowl and place the dough in the refrigerator for 2 hours.

After 2 hours, mix all filling ingredients together. Flour a board and roll out the pastry dough to ¼-inch thickness. Cut the dough into squares. Put a tablespoonful of filling in the middle of each square, fold one corner over to make a triangle, and pinch the edges together. Set the apple pastries on a greased cookie sheet, cover with a tea towel, and set in a cozy place for 2 hours. Then preheat the oven to 350° F. and bake for about 20 minutes or until light golden brown.

Mix the powdered sugar with the few drops of lemon juice. When the pastries have cooled, drizzle this mixture over each one. Makes 36 pastries.

Flower Pot Walnut Bread

Baking this bread in a flower pot gives it a pleasant shape.

I cup whole wheat flour
3 cups all-purpose flour
2 teaspoons baking powder
I teaspoon baking soda
½ cup sugar
2 teaspoons cinnamon
4 eggs
I ½ cups chunky applesauce
½ cup plain yogurt
½ cup margarine or butter, melted
4 tablespoons apple juice concentrate
I cup walnuts, chopped
I cup raisins

Combine flours, baking powder, baking soda, sugar, and cinnamon in a bowl. In a separate bowl, beat the eggs with the applesauce, yogurt, margarine, and apple juice. Add the walnuts and raisins. Stir all ingredients together until well mixed. Grease two clean clay flower pots. To cure the pots, place them in a cold oven and turn the oven to 350° F. Leave the pots in the oven for 45 minutes, then remove them and allow them to cool before using. Place waxed paper or greased foil in the bottom of each pot to plug the hole and help the bread come out easier. Grease the pots again and dust them inside with flour. Fill the pots with batter and return them to the hot oven. Bake for I hour and 10 minutes or until a skewer comes out clean. Remove bread when cool to the touch. Makes 2 loaves.

Waffles with Ground Walnuts

3 cups flour
¾ cup wheat germ
¼ cup sugar
2 teaspoons baking powder
I ½ cups walnuts or almonds, ground fine
2 cups milk
I teaspoon vanilla
I ½ cups sour cream
5 eggs
Margarine or butter for frying

In a large bowl, blend all dry ingredients. Add the milk, vanilla, and sour cream and beat until smooth. Add the eggs, one at a time, until the batter is thick. Let the batter sit for 20 minutes before using.

Heat the waffle iron, using a little margarine to grease the surface of the iron. Then pour in approximately ¼ cup of batter.

The waffles are done when golden brown on both sides. Serve with butter and powdered sugar or jam, whipped cream, fresh fruit, syrup, or anything you like. Makes 12 waffles.

Shown opposite:
Waffles with Ground Walnuts.

Walnut Pancakes with Orange Butter Sauce

ORANGE BUTTER SAUCE
4 oranges
8 tablespoons butter
¼ cup sugar
½ cup orange liqueur

PANCAKES
¾ cup whole wheat flour
2 ½ cups all-purpose flour
¾ cup sugar
¾ cup walnuts, ground fine
3 cups milk
5 eggs, separated
2 teaspoons vanilla
Oil for frying

In a small pot, melt the butter. Grate the rind of two of the oranges and add to the butter. Juice all four oranges, using a juicer or your hands, and add to the pot. Add the remaining sauce ingredients and let simmer for 10 minutes.

While the sauce is simmering, blend the flours, sugar, and the ground nuts. Beat in the milk, egg yolks, and vanilla. In a separate bowl, beat the egg whites until stiff, and fold into the batter. Heat just enough oil to cover the bottom of a frying pan. Pour ½ cup of batter at a time into the frying pan and fry the pancakes on both sides.

Serve the sauce warm over the pancakes. Makes 25 pancakes.

Walnut Raspberry Bread

2 cups all-purpose flour
½ cup whole wheat flour
1 cup sugar
1 ½ teaspoons baking soda
1 egg, beaten
3 tablespoons butter, melted
¾ cup milk
1 teaspoon vanilla
1 cup walnuts, chopped
1 cup fresh raspberries
¼ cup coarsely chopped walnuts
   for topping

Preheat oven to 375° F. In a bowl, mix the flours, sugar, and baking soda. Add the egg, melted butter, milk, and vanilla and mix well. Stir in the 1 cup of chopped walnuts and the raspberries. Pour into a greased 5x9-inch loaf pan. Sprinkle the remaining walnuts on top and bake for 45 minutes or until a fork comes out clean. Makes 1 loaf of bread.

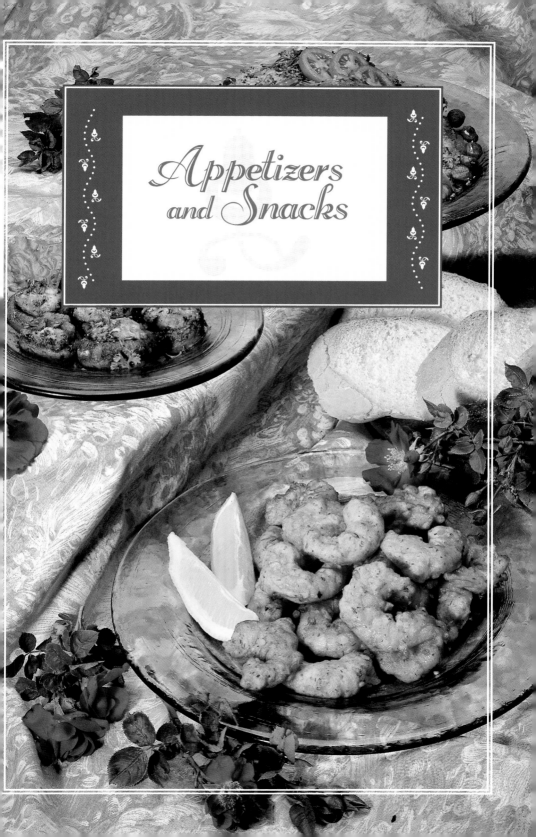

Appetizers
and Snacks

Almond Candy

3 cups slivered almonds
1 cup powdered sugar
12 ounces sweet chocolate

Preheat the oven to 375° F. Place the almond slivers on a baking tray and sprinkle them with powdered sugar. Bake for 15 minutes and then let cool. Melt the chocolate in a double boiler or use two pans, the smaller one for the chocolate. Place the smaller pan into a larger pan filled with water. Melt the chocolate over medium heat. Then quickly stir in the almonds. Using a teaspoon, place clusters on greased foil or waxed paper to cool. Makes 24 candies.

Cheeseball with Almonds

2 cups shredded cheddar cheese
1 cup shredded Edam cheese
1 cup dates, pitted and chopped
¾ cup butter, soft
2 ½ tablespoons brandy
¾ cup sliced almonds,
   toasted (see page x)

Mix the cheeses with the dates and stir in the butter and brandy. Knead the ingredients until well blended. Then form the mixture into a ball. Roll the ball in the sliced almonds and wrap it in foil or plastic. Let the cheeseball sit overnight in a cool place.

Shown previous page:
Almond Shrimp, page 14.

Almond Peanut Brittle

3 cups sugar
1 ½ cups light corn syrup
¾ cup water
1 ½ cups raw whole peanuts,
   skins removed
1 ½ cups almonds, blanched
3 tablespoons butter

Grease or butter a baking sheet well. In a large saucepan, combine the sugar, corn syrup, and water. Stir over low heat until sugar is completely dissolved. Turn the heat up a bit and stir until the mixture is light brown. Turn off the heat and quickly add the nuts and butter, stirring them in well. Pour the mixture onto the greased baking sheet and let it cool. Break the brittle into pieces and store in an airtight container.

Burnt Almonds

2 cups sugar
¾ cup water
2 cups whole almonds

In a skillet, heat the sugar and the water. Let this simmer until it is light brown. Stir in the almonds and continue stirring for another 10 minutes. Make sure the almonds are completely coated with the syrup. Spread the mixture on a buttered cookie sheet. Let it cool, then break into pieces.

Chicken Appetizer

CHICKEN
¾ cup butter or oil
1 egg
½ cup cornflake crumbs
½ cup almonds, chopped fine
½ cup fine bread crumbs
2 teaspoons oregano
2 teaspoons thyme
2 teaspoons cumin
3 whole chicken breasts,
    each cut into 12 cubes

DIP SAUCE
¾ cup sour cream
2 tablespoons mustard
8 drops Tabasco sauce
¼ teaspoon pepper

Preheat oven to 400° F. Melt the butter or oil. Remove from the heat and whisk in the egg. In a separate bowl, mix all dry ingredients. Dip the chicken cubes into the egg and butter mixture, then into the bread crumb mixture. Place the breaded cubes on a cookie tray. Place the tray in a hot oven for 15–20 minutes or until the chicken cubes are crisp and tender. Combine all sauce ingredients and serve on the side. Makes 36 pieces.

Nut Party Mix

2 cups almonds
2 cups cashews, blanched
½ cup pine nuts
2 cups hazelnuts
6 tablespoons vegetable oil
⅓ cup sweet vermouth
1 cup raisins
¼ cup shredded coconut
Salt

Preheat oven to 350° F. Spread the nuts out on a cookie sheet and bake until slightly brown. Let them cool.
    In a saucepan, combine the vermouth and raisins. Simmer until the vermouth has evaporated, then let raisins cool. Stir the browned nuts and the oil together on the cookie sheet, then toast in oven for 10 minutes. Combine the nuts with all other ingredients and add salt to taste. Store in an airtight container. Makes 7 cups.

Toasted Almonds

2 cups almonds, blanched, unblanched,
    slivered or whole
2 tablespoons butter, melted

Preheat oven to 350° F. Spread the nuts on a cookie tray and brush them with the melted butter. Place in the oven; stir occasionally. Toast 10 minutes or until golden brown, then remove from the oven. Let the nuts cool and store them in an airtight container. Makes 2 cups.

Almond Shrimp

1 cup almonds, ground
1 cup flour
½ teaspoon salt
¼ teaspoon pepper
¼ teaspoon dill
3 tablespoons lemon juice
1 egg
1 cup white wine
1 pound shrimp, peeled and
    deveined, tails left on
4 cups vegetable oil for frying
1 lemon, cut into wedges

Combine all ingredients except the
shrimp, vegetable oil, and lemon;
blend well.

   Heat the oil. Dip the shrimp in
the almond batter and, a few at a time,
fry in the oil. Drain on paper towels.
Serve the shrimp hot with the lemon
wedges. Serves 4.

Tomato Chutney with Almonds

12-ounce can crushed tomatoes
1 ½ cups cider vinegar
1 ½ cups sugar
1 teaspoon crushed garlic
1 ½ teaspoons salt
1 ½ teaspoons pepper
½ teaspoon cayenne pepper
¼ cup raisins
¼ cup slivered almonds, blanched

In a saucepan, combine all the
ingredients except the raisins and the
almonds. Over low heat, let this chutney
simmer for 2 hours. Add the raisins and
almonds; let simmer for another 20
minutes. Let cool before serving. Makes
2 cups.

Coconut Milk

*This recipe can be used in curry and rice recipes
such as those on pages 42 and 24.*

2 cups shredded coconut
2 cups boiling water

Place the coconut in a food processor,
add the water, and blend for 4 minutes.
Strain through cheesecloth or a strainer
and pour into a storage container.
Keep refrigerated.

Eggplant Dip with Cashews

3 medium eggplants
1 cup olive oil
4 slices of white bread, crusts cut off
2 teaspoons crushed garlic
6 tablespoons cider vinegar
¾ cup cashews, chopped fine
¼ teaspoon salt
¼ teaspoon pepper
Dash of Tabasco sauce

Preheat oven to 350° F. With a fork, prick many holes in each of the eggplants. Bake them in the oven for about 50 minutes. Let them cool, then scoop out the meat. Discard the peel. Combine the eggplant and the other ingredients in a food processor or blender; blend well. Chill before serving. Makes 3 cups.

Cashews

The cashew nut is the kernel of a kidney-shaped fruit that grows on a tropical evergreen found in Africa, South America and parts of Asia. The dark rind around the nut is extremely acidic and, according to an old folk remedy, can be used to cure warts and ringworm. The cashew is also related to poison ivy, and its shell contains an irritating poison that can cause skin blisters if the raw shell is touched. Roasting removes the poison from the shell.

Hazelnut Candy

4 cups whole hazelnuts
12 ounces sweet chocolate

Preheat oven to 375° F. Place the hazelnuts on a cookie sheet and toast them in the oven for 15 minutes. Then let them cool. Melt the chocolate in a double boiler or use two pans, the smaller one containing the chocolate, the larger one containing water. Melt over medium heat. Put the toasted hazelnuts in a bowl and pour the melted chocolate over them. Using two spoons, place clusters of three or four hazelnuts on greased foil or waxed paper. Let them cool. Makes 20 candies.

Hot Hazelnut Chocolate

4 ounces semi-sweet chocolate
4 ½ cups milk
¼ cup sugar
2 cups heavy cream
3 cups strong coffee
¾ cup hazelnut liqueur
5 tablespoons finely chopped hazelnuts

In a saucepan, combine the semi-sweet chocolate, milk, and sugar. Stir over low heat for 10 minutes, then add 1 ½ cups of the heavy cream, the coffee, and the hazelnut liqueur. Heat carefully, making sure not to boil. Beat the remaining ½ cup cream until stiff. Pour the chocolate into cups, top each with a spoonful of cream, and sprinkle chopped hazelnuts on top. Serve hot. Serves 8–10.

Spicy Pecans

2 tablespoons butter
2 cups pecans
½ teaspoon ginger
1 teaspoon paprika
¼ teaspoon salt
2 teaspoons soy sauce

Melt the butter in a saucepan. Pour in the pecans, then add the spices and the soy sauce. Over medium heat, stir for 10 minutes. Remove from heat, cool, and serve. Makes 2 cups.

Pecans

Native to the United States, pecans were roasted and ground in stews by Native Americans. The word *pecan* is kin to words in several Indian languages for "nut having hard shell to crack." Pecans are also grown in Australia, Israel, and South Africa. The tree can grow to 180 feet tall and can take up to twenty years to produce a profitable crop.

The pecan is high in vitamin A and protein. Besides cakes and pies, I have added them to chutney recipes in this book.

Piñon Nut Egg Rolls

2 cups bean sprouts
1 cup grated carrot
1 cup thinly sliced cabbage
1 cup chopped green onions
1 cup water chestnuts, chopped
½ cup piñon nuts, chopped
1 ½ cups small shrimp, cooked
    and peeled
6 tablespoons soy sauce
5 tablespoons dry sherry
2 teaspoons peeled and finely
    chopped fresh ginger root
30 egg roll wrappers
1 teaspoon cornstarch
2 tablespoons water
Oil for frying

In a bowl, combine the vegetables with the nuts and shrimp, soy sauce, sherry, and ginger root. Place 2 heaping tablespoons of filling on each egg roll wrapper. Mix the cornstarch with the water, then brush on the edges of each wrapper to help seal the egg rolls. Tightly wrap each egg roll, tucking in the ends. Then heat enough oil to cover the egg rolls and fry two egg rolls at a time for 4 minutes or until golden brown. Serve hot with soy or mustard sauce. Makes 30 egg rolls.

Stuffed Grape Leaves with Pine Nuts

Stuffed grape leaves taste great with zadziky (see recipe on page 50 and substitute ¼ teaspoon dill with ½ teaspoon of mint). In Greece they are eaten with or without a meat filling.

¼ cup olive oil
1 pound ground beef (optional)
2 cups short-grain rice
1 large onion, chopped fine
3 large ripe tomatoes, chopped fine
¼ cup parsley, chopped fine
¾ cup pine nuts, chopped
3 teaspoons cumin
3 teaspoons lemon juice
3 tablespoons chopped fresh mint
Salt and pepper to taste
1 jar grape leaves (or steam 40 fresh
  ones to soften them)

In a skillet, heat the oil, add the ground beef, and brown. Add the rice and onion and simmer for 5 minutes. Stir in all other ingredients except the grape leaves. Lay a grape leaf flat and put 1 ½ tablespoons of the stuffing on the leaf. Fold the sides in first and then wrap into a tight package. Place in a heavy-bottomed pot. Continue. Place the stuffed leaves tightly together until the first layer is completed. Start the next layer. When you have used up all of the stuffing, place a plate on top to hold the stuffed grape leaves down and fill the pot with water. Add a teaspoon of salt, place on the stove, and bring to a slow boil. Simmer for 1 ½ hours, making sure to replenish the water if it evaporates below the plate. Serve hot or cold. Makes 40.

Stuffed Mushrooms with Piñon Nuts

20 large mushrooms
8 tablespoons olive oil
1 small onion, chopped fine
1 teaspoon crushed garlic
2 tablespoons chopped parsley
¼ pound Italian sausage
¼ cup piñon nuts, chopped fine
1 teaspoon salt
½ teaspoon pepper
1 egg
4 slices of crustless bread, soaked
  in 8 teaspoons water
4 teaspoons oil or butter
¼ cup grated Parmesan cheese

Preheat oven to 400° F. Rinse the mushrooms and remove the stems. In the oil, sauté the chopped onion until clear. Remove from heat. Add the garlic, parsley, sausage, piñon nuts, salt, pepper, and egg. Squeeze the water out of the bread and mix the bread in, blending well. Using a teaspoon, fill the mushrooms with the filling. Brush the mushrooms with oil or melted butter, then roll each in Parmesan cheese. Place on a cookie sheet and bake for 25 minutes. Makes 20.

Pâté with Pistachios

This pâté is best served on dark bread with pickled cucumbers and beets.

1 ½ cups sliced mushrooms
1 ½ sticks butter
1 onion, minced
½ cup brandy
2 pounds chicken liver
1 ½ cups ground pork
3 eggs
3 potatoes, boiled
1 ½ teaspoons thyme
1 teaspoon pepper
1 ½ teaspoons salt
½ cup pistachio nuts, chopped fine
    (walnuts can be substituted)
1 cup parsley, chopped fine

Preheat oven to 350° F. In a frying pan, saute the mushrooms in the butter until golden. Using a slotted spoon, remove the mushrooms and place them in a bowl, then add the onion to the pan. Sauté the onion until transparent. Into a blender, pour the brandy, sautéed onions, and chicken liver. Purée, then add the ground pork, eggs, boiled potatoes, and spices. Blend well, until batter is completely smooth. Pour half the pâté mix into a greased tureen or two greased loaf pans. Place the mushrooms on top and sprinkle with the pistachio nuts and parsley. Pour the rest of the pâté on top of the mushrooms, parsley, and nuts. Fold foil tightly around the tureen and place it in a larger pan of hot water. Bake in the oven for 1 hour and 30 minutes, or until pâté comes away from the sides of the pan. Remove the foil and bake for another 15 minutes. Let the pâté cool overnight in the refrigerator before you remove it from the baking tureen or pan. Makes one large or two small patties.

Pistachios

A favorite of the Queen of Sheba, the pistachio nut is originally from Asia. It can also be found in the Middle East, Mediterranean countries, Texas, California, and Arizona. The Greeks called the pistachio *egines*, which means "the beginning." A Greek island, Egina, is named after the nut.

Pistachio trees are either male or female. A female tree needs a male tree nearby so that pollen can be provided for the flowers.

In Western countries, pistachios are used mostly for snacks and in ice cream. In Greece, the nut is used in pastries such as baklava. It is rich in potassium.

Salmon Mousse

2 pounds fresh or frozen salmon steaks
3 slices lemon
½ teaspoon peppercorns
1 teaspoon salt
1 bay leaf
1 cup water
2 envelopes gelatin
5 tablespoons lemon juice
8 tablespoons white wine
1 tablespoon finely chopped onion
1 cup mayonnaise
1 ¼ cups heavy cream
1 cup watercress, chopped (save
   some nice pieces for garnish)
1 cup pistachios, ground
2 hard-boiled eggs, peeled and sliced
¼ cup mayonnaise for garnish

Put the salmon steaks in a pot of boiling water and add the lemon slices, pepper-corns, salt, and bay leaf. Turn the heat down and simmer until the fish meat comes loose from the bone (about 8 minutes). Drain the water and spices. Let the fish cool before removing the meat. Discard the bones and skin.

Boil 1 cup of water and dissolve the gelatin, then add the lemon juice and white wine. Pour this into a food processor or blender. Add the salmon meat, onion, and mayonnaise; blend quickly. Stir in the cream. Pour half of the salmon mixture into a mold. Spread the watercress, pistachios, and eggs on top of that, then pour the remaining salmon mixture on top of the watercress. Place in the refrigerator for 5 hours or overnight. Decorate with sprigs of watercress and, using a pastry tube, the mayonnaise. Serves up to 20.

Avocado Walnut Dip

3 ripe avocados
4 tablespoons lemon juice
¼ teaspoon salt
Pinch of black pepper
Pinch of red pepper
½ teaspoon ground garlic
1 tablespoon flat chopped parsley
2 tablespoons sour cream
2 medium tomatoes, chopped
4 sprigs green onion, chopped
1 ½ cups walnuts, chopped
Dash of gin or Tabasco sauce

Peel the avocados, then, in a bowl, mash them with a fork. Stir in the lemon juice and the spices. Add the remaining ingredients and stir until well blended. Chill for 1 hour before serving.
Makes 3 cups.

Spiced Walnuts

½ cup butter
¾ cup sugar
4 cups walnuts
I ½ teaspoons cinnamon
¾ teaspoon ginger
¾ teaspoon nutmeg
I pinch cardamom
I pinch salt

In a skillet, melt the butter. Add the
sugar and the walnuts. Stir for I5
minutes over medium heat. Mix the
spices and sift them over the walnuts.
Spread the walnuts on a greased cookie
sheet. Let cool, break into pieces, and
store. Makes 4 cups.

Spinach Walnut Dip

2 cups sour cream
I cup mayonnaise
I package dry leek soup
¼ teaspoon garlic powder
10-ounce package frozen spinach,
   chopped, thawed, and drained
½ cup finely chopped parsley
½ cup finely chopped green onions
I ½ cups chopped walnuts

In a large bowl, combine the sour cream
and the mayonnaise. Add the leek soup
and garlic and stir. Add the remaining
ingredients and mix well. Cover and
refrigerate overnight. Makes 6 cups.

Swiss Cheese Dip

3 slices dried bread, diced
¾ cup diced Swiss cheese
4 ounces cream cheese
¼ teaspoon crushed garlic
¼ cup orange juice
¼ cup walnuts
Pepper to taste

Place all ingredients in a blender or
food processor. Blend well, then chill.
Garnish with whole walnuts and parsley.
Makes I ½ cups.

Walnut Garlic Spread

I cup walnuts, ground fine
I teaspoon crushed garlic
4 slices white bread, crusts removed
I teaspoon finely chopped parsley
I tablespoon olive oil
2 tablespoons cider vinegar
Salt and pepper to taste

In a bowl, combine the walnuts with the
garlic. Soak the bread in water, then
squeeze out the excess. Mix the bread
and parsley with the walnuts and garlic.
Then, little by little, stir in the oil and
vinegar and add salt and pepper to taste.
Store in refrigerator. Makes I cup.

Soups, Salads, and Side Dishes

Almond Soup

3 tablespoons butter
2 tablespoons flour
½ cup milk
3 cups chicken broth
1 ½ cups almonds,
    blanched and ground
1 whole onion
1 bay leaf
1 cup heavy cream
¼ cup slivered almonds,
    toasted (see page x)

In a saucepan, melt the butter, then stir in the flour. Gradually stir in the milk. Let simmer, continuously stirring until smooth. Little by little, stir in the chicken broth. Add the ground almonds, onion, and bay leaf. Let simmer for 10 minutes, then remove the onion and the bay leaf. Stir in the cream. Ladle into bowls, sprinkle with the toasted almonds, and serve. Serves 4.

Zucchini and Cherry Tomatoes with Toasted Almonds

2 tablespoons butter
¾ cup slivered almonds
3 tablespoons olive oil
2 pints cherry tomatoes
4 medium yellow zucchini, cleaned
    and cut into ½-inch slices
1 teaspoon basil
1 teaspoon chopped parsley
1 teaspoon oregano
¾ teaspoon salt
½ teaspoon pepper

In a frying pan, melt the butter. Add the almonds and stir for 7 minutes. Remove the almonds and drain on a paper towel. Add the olive oil, whole tomatoes, and zucchini. Stir over medium heat until the tomatoes are soft, but not cracked (about 10 minutes). Sprinkle the vegetables with the spices and almonds and serve immediately. Serves 6.

Shown previous page:
Chicken and Fruit Salad with Cashews, page 25.

Shown opposite:
Zucchini and Tomatoes with Toasted Almonds.

Vegetables and Almonds in Sherry

4 tablespoons butter or margarine
1 medium onion, sliced
2 cups snow peas
4 carrots, peeled and cut into strips
1 cup slivered almonds
¼ cup cooking sherry
Salt and pepper to taste

In a skillet, sauté the onion in the butter for 4 minutes. Add the snow peas, carrots, almonds, and sherry; sauté for 4 more minutes. Add salt and pepper, then serve. Serves 4.

Coconut Rice

3 tablespoons butter
1 ½ cups long-grain rice
5 whole cloves
½ teaspoon salt
2 whole cardamom pods, crushed
1 teaspoon cumin
4 cups coconut milk (see recipe on page 14)

In a thick-bottomed casserole, melt the butter. Stir in the rice and spices, then sauté and continue stirring for 8 minutes. Pour the coconut milk into the rice, cover with a lid, and simmer for 15–20 minutes over low heat.

Brazil Nut Fries

5 tablespoons butter or margarine
1 medium onion, chopped
3 tablespoons flour
1 cup milk
Salt and pepper to taste
1 egg
¾ cup Brazil nuts, chopped fine
½ cup wheat germ
1 ½ cups bread crumbs
1 egg, beaten
5 tablespoons bread crumbs
Olive oil for frying

Melt the butter and sauté the onion until clear. Stir in the flour, then gradually add the milk and salt and pepper. Beat in 1 egg, then mix in the nuts, wheat germ, and 1 ½ cups bread crumbs. Cool.

Form the dough into small, flat pancakes. Dip each pancake in egg, then in the 5 tablespoons of bread crumbs. In heated olive oil, fry on both sides until golden brown. Serves 4.

Chicken and Fruit Salad with Cashews

This salad is attractive and delicious served chilled on a bed of lettuce with rolls and butter.

SALAD

1 whole baking chicken
2 cups grapes, halved
3 kiwi fruit, peeled and diced
1 14-ounce can pineapple chunks
2 cups strawberries, hulled and halved
1 ½ cups cashews
1 head butter lettuce

MAYONNAISE DRESSING

1 cup mayonnaise
1 cup sour cream
1 teaspoon lemon juice
½ teaspoon freshly ground pepper
½ teaspoon salt

Preheat the oven to 350° F. Rinse the chicken inside and out and place in a greased pan. Bake in the oven for 1 ½ hours. Let cool before pulling the meat off. Discard the skin and bones; cut the meat into bite-sized chunks. In a bowl, gently fold the chicken pieces in with the fruit and nuts.

Blend the dressing ingredients. Either carefully mix the dressing into the salad or serve it on the side. Serves 6.

Lobster Salad with Cashew Nuts

SALAD

2-pound lobster, or 1 pound
  packaged lobster meat
1 head butter lettuce
2 avocados, peeled and diced
4 small tomatoes, cut into wedges
4 bunches arugula stems, trimmed
1 cucumber, peeled and diced
1 cup fresh cashews

DILL DRESSING

8 tablespoons vegetable oil
2 tablespoons lemon juice
2 tablespoons finely chopped parsley
3 tablespoons finely chopped
  green onion
4 tablespoons finely chopped fresh dill
½ tablespoon minced garlic

Fill a large pot with water and bring it to a boil. Add the live lobster and 1 teaspoon salt and boil until the lobster is bright red (about 12 minutes). Remove the lobster from the water and let it cool, then remove the tail and claw meat. Cut all the meat into cubes. Arrange the lobster meat on a bed of lettuce along with the avocados, tomatoes, arugula stems, cucumber, and cashews.

Combine all dressing ingredients and chill. Pour over the salad. Serves 4.

Hazelnut and Artichoke Salad with Watercress Dressing

SALAD
1 ½ cups hazelnuts
1 head romaine lettuce
1 bunch spinach
6-ounce can marinated artichoke
  hearts, quartered
2 tomatoes, cut into wedges
6 radishes, cut into thin slices
6 ham slices, cut lengthwise into strips
6 eggs, hard-boiled, peeled, and
  quartered

WATERCRESS DRESSING
2 tablespoons lemon juice
1 tablespoon tarragon vinegar
½ cup olive oil
1 teaspoon salt
⅛ teaspoon pepper
1 cup watercress, chopped fine

Preheat the oven to 375° F. Toast the hazelnuts for 15 minutes on a baking sheet in the oven. Rinse and dry the lettuce and spinach and tear the large leaves into bite-sized pieces. Arrange all the vegetables, lettuce, ham, and boiled eggs on six individual plates. Mix the dressing ingredients in a small bowl and pour over the salads. Sprinkle the warm hazelnuts on top and serve immediately. Serves 6.

Bulgur Hazelnut Pilaf

2 cups hot water
2 cups bulgur
1 ¼ cups olive oil
3 teaspoons cumin
1 teaspoon crushed garlic
1 teaspoon salt
½ teaspoon pepper
¼ cup lemon juice
1 ½ cups hazelnuts, chopped
½ cup finely chopped red onion
1 bunch finely chopped green onions
1 cup chopped celery
2 cups parsley, chopped fine
10 ripe tomatoes, chopped

Pour the water into a bowl. Add the bulgur and let it sit for 20 minutes. In a separate bowl, combine the olive oil with the spices and lemon juice, and stir. Add the remaining ingredients, then add to the bulgur. Cover, refrigerate for 2 hours, then serve. Serves 12.

Macadamia Nuts

The macadamia tree grows to be 40 feet tall. This tree was brought to Hawaii from Australia, and the nuts are also called Australian nuts. They are used mostly in cakes, candy, and ice cream.

Potato Salad with Macadamia Nuts

10 small new potatoes
½ onion, cut into thin slices
2 cups snow peas
1 cup corn kernels
8 tablespoons olive oil
4 tablespoons lemon juice
2 teaspoons mustard
2 teaspoons dill
1 teaspoon basil
¾ cup macadamia nuts,
    sliced or chopped

Scrub the potatoes and slice them into ¼-inch slices. Simmer the slices in salted water (enough to cover the potatoes) until they are almost tender. Add the onion, snow peas, and corn kernels and bring to a boil. Boil for 3 minutes, then remove from the heat. Drain and place vegetables in a bowl. In a smaller bowl, mix the remaining ingredients, except the nuts, and pour this mixture over the vegetables. Refrigerate overnight. Just before serving, add the nuts and salt and pepper to taste. Serves 6.

Oriental Chicken Salad with Peanuts

SALAD
5 tablespoons sesame seeds
½ teaspoon vegetable oil
1 cup water
2 stalks celery, chopped
2 cups snow peas
2 chicken breasts, cooked, cut into strips
6 green onions, chopped fine
1 cup raw peanuts
4 teaspoons finely chopped cilantro
2 cups shredded cabbage

ORIENTAL DRESSING
¾ cup plain yogurt
¼ cup mayonnaise
3 tablespoons honey
1 teaspoon grated ginger root
Pepper and salt to taste

In a skillet, brown the sesame seeds in oil and place them in a salad bowl. In a saucepan, bring the water to a boil, and add the snow peas and celery. Turn the heat down and let the vegetables simmer for about 3 minutes. Remove them from the water and add to the sesame seeds. Add the chicken, green onions, peanuts, cilantro, and cabbage and mix.

   In a bowl, combine all dressing ingredients. Just before serving, pour the dressing over the salad. Serves 4.

Black Bean Pecan Salad

2 cups black beans
2 tablespoons shortening
1 teaspoon onion powder
2 garlic cloves, chopped
1 teaspoon rosemary
4 cups chicken stock
2 celery stalks, chopped into small pieces
1 white onion, chopped into small pieces
2 cans artichoke hearts (save the marinade)
2 carrots, chopped into small pieces
1 teaspoon sage
Salt and pepper to taste
1 cup pecans, chopped
3 tablespoons chopped parsley
¼ cup olive oil
4 tablespoons cider vinegar

Rinse and drain the beans. In a large saucepan, bring 10 cups of water to a boil; add the beans. Let them boil for 5 minutes, turn off the heat, and let them sit for 4 hours. Drain the water and rinse the beans, then pour them back into the pot. Add the shortening, onion powder, garlic, rosemary, and chicken stock. Let the beans simmer until tender and drain the chicken stock. Add the vegetables, spices, pecans, parsley, oil, vinegar, and salt and pepper to taste. Serve chilled. Serves 6.

Rhubarb Pecan Chutney

4 cups chopped rhubarb
5 cooking apples, peeled and diced
2 cups brown sugar
1 ½ cups cider vinegar
1 cup raisins
1 cup pecans, chopped
1 teaspoon minced garlic
½ teaspoon finely chopped ginger root
1 teaspoon allspice
1 teaspoon cumin
⅛ teaspoon red pepper

In a thick-bottomed saucepan, combine all ingredients. Simmer on low heat for 2 hours, stirring occasionally. Cool before serving. Store in refrigerator or freeze. Makes 4 cups.

Pine Nuts

Pine nuts, or piñon nuts as they are called in the southwestern U. S., have been used for centuries as a reliable food source by the American Indians of the Southwest, as well as by inhabitants of Mediterranean countries and the Baltics.

These nuts are high in fat and become rancid if not stored properly. The pine nut is actually the kernel of a seed found in pine cones. The cones are collected during the late fall or winter, then spread out on a blanket to dry so that the seeds can be easily shaken loose. They are 66 percent fat and 14 percent protein.

Cold Asparagus Soup with Pine Nuts

4 tablespoons butter
3 stalks celery, chopped
1 onion, chopped
1 pound asparagus, chopped
  and tips set aside
2 potatoes, peeled and diced
1 cup chopped broccoli stems
4 cups chicken broth
1 ½ cups half and half
6 teaspoons gin
½ cup heavy cream, whipped
¼ cup pine nuts, toasted (see page x)

In the butter, sauté the celery, onion, asparagus, potatoes, and broccoli. Add the chicken broth. Let simmer for 15 minutes, then purée in a blender or food processor. Add the half and half and the gin, then chill for 4 hours. Steam the asparagus tips and chill. Just before serving, garnish each bowl with a table-spoon of whipped cream, some pine nuts, and asparagus tips. Soup may be stored in refrigerator in the blender. Serves 8.

Lemon Rice with Piñon Nuts

½ cup finely chopped onions
Grated rind of 1 lemon
3 tablespoons olive oil
2 ¼ cups long-grain rice
6 cups chicken stock
¾ cup grated Parmesan cheese
1 cup piñon nuts
¼ cup parsley, chopped
Salt and pepper to taste

In a heavy-bottomed pot, sauté the onion and lemon rind in the olive oil for about 7 minutes. Add the rice and pour in the chicken stock. Over low heat, let the rice mixture simmer until it is done (about 20 minutes). Stir in the Parmesan cheese and the piñon nuts. Sprinkle with parsley and serve immediately. Serves 6.

Piñon Nut and Avocado Shrimp Salad

SALAD
2 ripe avocados
4 teaspoons lemon juice
2 tomatoes, diced
½ cup black olives, chopped
½ cup piñon nuts
1 ½ cups small shrimp, cooked
   and peeled

DRESSING
3 tablespoons olive oil
3 tablespoons red wine vinegar
½ teaspoon salt
¼ teaspoon pepper
¼ teaspoon turmeric
½ teaspoon Tabasco sauce
2 tablespoons chopped parsley

Cut the avocados in half, scoop out the meat, and rub the inside of the shells with a little lemon juice. Set the shells aside. In a bowl, dice the meat and sprinkle with the remaining lemon juice. Add the tomatoes, olives, piñon nuts, and shrimp. Gently mix.

In a separate bowl, mix the olive oil, vinegar, and spices. Spoon the salad into the avocado shells, sprinkle with the dressing, and serve cold. Serves 4.

Stuffed Tomatoes

4 medium tomatoes
3 tablespoons olive oil
½ cup long-grain rice
1 onion, chopped fine
1 squash, chopped
1 teaspoon crushed garlic
½ teaspoon cumin
¼ teaspoon cinnamon
½ teaspoon salt
½ cup piñon nuts, chopped
2 cups chicken stock
4 tablespoons chopped parsley
½ cup grated mozzarella cheese

Preheat oven to 350° F. Cut the tops off the tomatoes and scoop out the meat. Cut the tomato meat into small cubes. In a skillet, heat the oil and sauté the rice with the onion, squash, spices, and piñon nuts. Sauté for 7 minutes. Add the chicken stock, tomato meat, and parsley. Using a spoon, scoop the mixture into the hollowed-out tomatoes. Sprinkle the grated mozzarella on top of the stuffed tomatoes. Bake for 50 minutes. Serves 4.

Turkish Rice with Pistachio Nuts

5 tablespoons butter
1 ½ cups long-grain rice
3 cups water
¼ teaspoon allspice
¼ teaspoon nutmeg
1 teaspoon salt
½ cup pistachio nuts, shelled
½ cup slivered or chopped
   almonds, blanched
½ cup raisins

In a skillet, melt the butter; then stir in
the rice. Over low heat, continue stirring
for 5 minutes. Add the water and the
spices, then simmer for 20 minutes. Mix
in the nuts and the raisins, then serve.
Serves 6.

Ham Salad with Walnuts

SALAD
1 pound asparagus
1 bunch spinach, leaves rinsed and torn
1 cup frozen green peas, defrosted
2 oranges, peeled and cut into chunks
2 cups strawberries, cleaned
   and cut in half
2 cups smoked ham, cut
   into strips or chunks
¾ cup walnuts

ORANGE DRESSING
½ cup sour cream
½ cup mayonnaise
2 tablespoons orange juice
Pepper, freshly ground

In boiling salted water, cook the
asparagus for 5 minutes. Remove
asparagus from the water, cool, and cut
into bite-sized chunks. In a bowl,
carefully toss all salad ingredients,
including the asparagus, together.
   In a small bowl, combine all dressing
ingredients. Pour the dressing over the
salad just before serving. Serves 6.

Nut Tater Tots

3 medium potatoes, peeled and boiled
3 tablespoons butter
1 cup chestnuts, chopped fine
1 cup walnuts or Brazil nuts,
    chopped fine
¾ cup heavy cream
3 eggs
1 tablespoon grated onion
Salt and pepper to taste
¾ cup bread crumbs
Olive oil for frying

In a bowl, mash the boiled potatoes. Stir in the butter, nuts, cream, 2 of the eggs, and onion. Add salt and pepper. Refrigerate for 1 hour. Form the potato dough into a long, sausage-shaped roll, then cut and shape into 16 little balls. Beat the remaining egg and dip each ball into the egg and roll it in the bread crumbs. Fry a few at a time in hot oil until golden brown. Serves 4.

Chestnuts

The chestnut tree grows to 100 feet in height and is found in Spain, Italy, and France. The leaves and bark of the chestnut tree can be used for medicinal purposes, and the nut itself contains less fat than other nuts.

Chestnuts are used in stews, sauces, desserts, and stuffings. To peel chestnuts, cut a cross the sides of the shells, then roast them in the oven at 375° F. for 8 minutes.

Flower Salad with Toasted Walnuts

This recipe uses fresh flowers from your garden. All flowers and leaves should be cleaned carefully.

SALAD
½ head young lettuce leaves
3 carrots, peeled into paper-thin strips
2 cups young dandelion leaves
2 pears, cut into thin slices
2 cups jicama, cut paper thin
4 tablespoons whole snapdragon flowers
4 tablespoons geranium petals
4 tablespoons nasturtium petals
4 tablespoons rose petals
4 tablespoons violet petals
1 cup walnuts, freshly toasted
    (pecans can be substituted)

DRESSING
2 cups strawberries
½ cup plain yogurt
4 tablespoons orange juice

Gently combine the lettuce leaves with the carrot strips, dandelion leaves, pears, and jicama. Divide onto six salad plates, top with the flower petals, and sprinkle the warm, toasted nuts over all.

Combine all dressing ingredients in a blender or food processor and purée. Serve the dressing on the side. Serves 6.

Shown opposite:
Flower Salad with Toasted Walnuts.

Potatoes with Cheese and Walnuts

4 large potatoes
2 tablespoons vegetable oil
4 tablespoons butter
¼ teaspoon salt
⅛ teaspoon pepper
I egg
2 tablespoons chives
I cup cream cheese
¾ cup walnuts, chopped fine
I cup grated mozzarella
   or cheddar cheese
½ cup grated Parmesan cheese

Preheat oven to 375° F. Scrub the potatoes and rub them with oil. Bake them in the oven for I hour or until tender inside. Remove from the oven and let cool a little. Leave the oven on. Cut a top lengthwise off each potato, scoop out the insides, and place the insides in a bowl. Set the potato shells aside. Add the butter, salt, pepper, egg, chives, and cream cheese. Beat with an electric mixer until fluffy. Stir in the walnuts. Fill the potato shells with the potato mixture; sprinkle with the mozzarella and Parmesan cheeses. Bake for another 20 minutes and serve hot. Serves 4.

Rotelle Noodles with Walnut Sauce

18 ounces rotelle noodles or other pasta
2 ½ cups walnuts
I egg yolk
I ¼ cups milk or half and half
4 tablespoons butter, melted
2 teaspoons salt
I teaspoon pepper
½ teaspoon crushed garlic
½ teaspoon rosemary, crushed
I teaspoon oregano

Cook pasta as directed on package. In a blender or food processor, combine all the other ingredients. Pour the sauce over the cooked pasta and quickly heat through. Serve hot. Serves 6.

Salad with Walnut-Poppy Seed Dressing

SALAD

6 medium tomatoes, cut into wedges
1 cucumber, peeled and sliced
6 radishes, sliced
1 head butter lettuce, torn
  into bite-sized pieces
1 medium red onion, sliced very thin

DRESSING

¼ cup walnuts
⅔ cup vegetable oil
Juice of 1 orange (¼ cup)
¼ cup lemon juice
3 tablespoons sugar
2 teaspoons grated red onion
1 teaspoon Dijon mustard
½ teaspoon salt
¼ teaspoon pepper
3 teaspoons poppy seeds

In a large bowl, combine all vegetables for the salad.

In a food processor or blender, combine all dressing ingredients until creamy. Serve the dressing on top of the salad. Serves 6.

Sliced Walnut Potatoes

These taste great topped with sour cream.

8 russet or other potatoes
1 cup walnuts, chopped fine
8 tablespoons butter, melted
Salt and pepper

Cut the potatoes into ¼-inch slices. Place slices in a bowl of cold water for ½ hour.

Preheat oven to 425° F. Drain the potatoes, transfer them to a greased baking pan, and pour half of the melted butter over them. Sprinkle with salt and pepper; bake the potatoes for 45 minutes. Flip the potatoes over, baste with the remaining butter, and sprinkle with the chopped walnuts. Bake for another 30 minutes. Serve immediately. Serves 6.

Spinach Walnut Tarts

DOUGH
1 ½ cups flour
¼ teaspoon salt
½ cup walnuts, ground
1 stick butter, at room temperature

FILLING
10-ounce package frozen spinach,
  thawed, drained, and chopped
1 ½ cups ricotta cheese
¼ cup grated Parmesan cheese
¼ teaspoon nutmeg
1 cup walnuts, chopped fine
3 eggs
4 tablespoons heavy cream
  or half and half
Salt and pepper

Preheat oven to 375° F. Mix the flour, salt, and ½ cup of walnuts. Knead in the butter and work the dough until it is smooth; use a little water if the dough is dry. On a lightly floured surface, roll out the dough. Use the dough to line a 9-inch pie pan. Prick holes in the bottom and bake the crust for 10 minutes.

In a bowl, combine the spinach, ricotta, Parmesan, nutmeg, and 1 cup of walnuts. In a smaller bowl, beat the eggs and cream together; add this to the spinach mixture and mix well. Sprinkle with salt and pepper, then stir. Pour this filling into the baked pie shell and bake for 45 minutes. Serves 6.

Zucchini Walnut Dish

2 teaspoons vegetable oil or butter
1 large onion, sliced
1 yellow pepper, cut into strips
1 ½ cups water
3 small yellow zucchini,
  cut into thin strips
3 small green zucchini,
  cut into thin strips
2 cups broccoli, cut into small bunches
3 potatoes, cut into ½-inch slices
½ teaspoon thyme
Salt and pepper to taste
½ cup olive oil
¼ cup raspberry or cider vinegar
¼ cup freshly grated Parmesan cheese
1 cup walnuts, chopped

In a pan, heat the oil. Add the onion and yellow pepper and sauté for 4 minutes. Add the water and the other vegetables and the spices. Let simmer on low heat until the potatoes are tender but not mushy.

Combine the oil and vinegar. Before serving, spoon the oil and vinegar over the vegetables, then sprinkle with the Parmesan cheese and the walnuts. Serve hot or cold. Serves 6.

Main Dishes

Almond Chicken in Tomato Rice

2 cups green beans
1 cup water
4 tablespoons vegetable oil
1 whole chicken, deboned and
    cut into pieces
1 medium onion, chopped
1 cup rice
14-ounce can crushed tomatoes
5 tablespoons tomato paste
1 teaspoon rosemary, crushed
1 teaspoon chili powder
Salt and pepper to taste
½ cup slivered almonds
4 tablespoons chopped parsley

Cook the green beans in the water for 20 minutes; set aside. In a heavy-bottomed pot, heat the oil, then fry the chicken and onion for 10 minutes. Add the rice, tomatoes, tomato paste, spices, and the cooked green beans and water. Over low heat, simmer for 45 minutes. Stir in the almonds and serve with the parsley sprinkled on top. Serves 6.

Tofu Stir-Fry with Almonds

4 tablespoons soy sauce
2 tablespoons honey
½ teaspoon pepper
1 pound tofu, cut into squares
2 tablespoons olive oil
1 onion, chopped fine
2 zucchini, cut into strips
2 carrots, cut into strips
1 cup snow peas
1 teaspoon very thinly sliced
    ginger root
1 cup slivered almonds
½ cup sesame seeds

Combine the soy sauce, honey, and pepper. Pour the sauce over the tofu until it is well coated.

Heat the oil and sauté the vegetables and ginger root for 5 minutes. In a separate pan, toast the almonds and sesame seeds. Mix the tofu with the vegetables and heat. Sprinkle the mixture with the sesame seeds and almonds. Serve immediately. Serves 4.

Shown previous page:
Walnut-Stuffed Beef Filet, page 62.

Red Snapper Salad with Toasted Almonds

2 cups water
1 medium onion, sliced
4 lemon slices
¼ cup parsley, chopped
1 bay leaf
½ teaspoon salt
¼ teaspoon large-grain pepper
1 ½ pounds red snapper filets
1 cup water
¼ cup finely chopped green onions
1 cup frozen peas
1 ½ cups small broccoli spears
¾ cup sliced almonds
4 lettuce leaves
1 tomato, cut into wedges
4 lemon wedges
1 teaspoon chopped dill weed

Pour the water into a large pot and add the onion, lemon, parsley, bay leaf, salt, and pepper. Bring to a boil, then add the fish filets. Cover the pan and turn the heat down to simmer for about 8 minutes. Remove the fish carefully and refrigerate until completely cool.

In a saucepan, add 1 cup water and stir in the green onions, peas, and broccoli spears. Simmer for 5 minutes.

Toast the almonds in a frying pan in a little oil or butter until light brown.

Place the cold fish on the lettuce leaves. Arrange the broccoli, peas, green onions, almonds, tomato wedges and lemon wedges around the fish. Sprinkle with dill and serve cold. Serves 4.

Sole Filets

For a complete meal, serve these filets with new potatoes and a tossed salad.

½ pound fresh or canned shrimp, peeled
10 tablespoons cream cheese
Juice of 1 lemon
Salt and pepper to taste
12 small or 6 large filets of sole
3 carrots, peeled and cut into strips
Sprigs of fresh dill or 1 ½ teaspoons
    dill, dried
2 eggs, beaten
½ cup bread crumbs
½ cup sliced almonds
¼ cup butter, melted

Preheat oven to 350° F. In a small bowl, combine the shrimp, cream cheese, lemon juice and salt and pepper. Spoon this mixture into the middle of the filets. Place a few carrot strips and a sprig of dill on top and roll the filets up. Tie with cotton string. Dip each filet into the egg, then into the combined bread crumbs and almond slices. Place the filets in a greased ovenproof dish, then pour the melted butter over them. Bake for about 20 minutes. Serve with lemon wedges. Serves 6.

Trout with Almond Sauce

FISH
4 small trout
2 tablespoons butter
1 ½ teaspoons dill
Salt and pepper
Juice of 1 lemon

ALMOND SAUCE
6 tablespoons butter
½ cup slivered almonds
2 tablespoons lemon juice

Preheat oven to 350° F. Rinse the fish inside and out and cut off the heads. Place the fish on a large piece of foil. Melt the butter, stir in the dill, salt and pepper, and lemon juice. Brush this over the fish. Place the remaining butter sauce inside the fish.

Wrap the foil tightly around the fish, place in a baking pan, and bake for 15 minutes or until the fish comes cleanly away from the bone.

In a saucepan, melt the butter. Over low heat, stir in the almonds, and simmer until they are golden brown. Stir in the lemon juice, and spread this over the fish just before serving. Serves 4.

Shown opposite:
Sole Filets, page 39.

Stuffed Eggplant

2 medium eggplants
1 ½ cups water, boiling
½ cup bulgur
3 tablespoons butter or oil
2 small onions, chopped
2 garlic cloves, chopped
2 tomatoes, chopped
1 cup Brazil nuts or walnuts, chopped fine
2 tablespoons chopped parsley
¼ teaspoon cumin
2 tablespoons lemon juice
Salt and pepper to taste
4 thick slices of provolone

Cut the eggplants in half lengthwise. Soak them in salt water for ½ hour. Pat dry and scoop out the meat, being careful not to break the skin. Set skins aside.

In a separate bowl, pour the boiling water over the bulgur.

Preheat oven to 350° F. In a skillet, heat the butter and sauté the onion and garlic with the tomatoes and eggplant meat until the eggplant is done. Mix this with the bulgur. Add the nuts, parsley, cumin, lemon juice, and salt and pepper. Scoop this mixture into the hollowed-out eggplant shells. Place the shells in a baking pan and fill the pan with 1 inch of water. Bake for 1 hour. While baking, if the eggplant shells appear dry inside, add a little butter or water. After 1 hour, place a slice of provolone on each half, then bake for another 15 minutes. Serves 4.

Chicken Curry with Cashews

Serve this dish with rice and chutney (see page 14 for recipe).

CURRY PASTE
2 tablespoons vegetable oil
1 small onion, chopped
1 teaspoon coriander
4 tablespoons minced lemon grass
2 teaspoons finely chopped garlic
2 teaspoons turmeric
2 teaspoons finely chopped fresh ginger
2 teaspoons ground cumin
½ teaspoon red pepper

CHICKEN
1 whole chicken
2 cups chicken stock
1 cup coconut milk
  (see recipe on page 14)
1 cup cashews
Salt to taste

In a food processor or blender, combine all the curry paste ingredients and blend to a paste.

Debone and cut the chicken into bite-sized pieces. In a saucepan, combine the curry paste with the chicken stock. Bring the mixture to a boil, then add the chicken. Simmer for 30 minutes, then add the coconut milk and cashews. Simmer for 10 minutes. Remove from heat and add salt to taste. Serves 4.

Stir-Fried Chicken with Cashews

4 teaspoons vegetable oil
1 tablespoon minced or thinly
  sliced garlic
1 tablespoon thinly sliced ginger root
1 onion, sliced
1 cup chopped celery
1 pound chicken breasts, skinned,
  deboned, and sliced into
  bite-sized chunks
1 cup thinly sliced carrots
1 ½ cups sugar peas
2 yellow zucchini, sliced thin lengthwise
2 tablespoons cooking sherry
1 ½ tablespoons soy sauce
1 ½ tablespoons cornstarch
1 cup cashews

In a pan, heat the oil and sauté the garlic, ginger root, onion, and celery on low heat for 5 minutes. Add the chicken. Simmer until the chicken is thoroughly cooked. Add the vegetables and simmer for 3 minutes more. In a small bowl, mix the sherry, soy sauce, and cornstarch. Add this and the cashews to the other ingredients and blend well. Cook for 5 minutes and serve hot with rice. Serves 4.

Fettuccine in Red Cashew Sauce

16-ounce can tomato paste
½ cup red wine
1 cup water
2 teaspoons finely chopped parsley
1 teaspoon crushed garlic
¼ teaspoon pepper
1 teaspoon oregano
1 bay leaf
4 teaspoons olive oil
8 mushrooms, chopped
1 onion, peeled and diced
2 carrots, peeled and diced
   in small pieces
2 zucchini, diced
2 celery stalks, diced
1 green pepper, diced
1 cup cashews
12 ounces fettuccine noodles
¼ cup fresh basil, chopped fine
½ cup grated Parmesan cheese
6 teaspoons butter, melted

In a pot, combine the tomato paste with the red wine and water. Add the parsley, garlic, pepper, oregano, and bay leaf. Bring to a slow boil, then reduce the heat. Simmer for 30 minutes. Add more water if necessary. In a skillet, heat the olive oil and sauté the mushrooms and the onion for 5 minutes. Remove from heat and add the remaining vegetables and the cashew nuts. Add this mixture to the tomato sauce and simmer for 15 minutes. While the vegetables simmer, cook the fettuccine for 12 minutes or as directed on the package. In a small bowl, combine the basil, Parmesan cheese, and melted butter. Drain the fettuccine and stir in the basil mixture. Remove the bay leaf and serve the vegetable sauce on top of the fettuccine. Serves 4 – 6.

Turkey with Chestnut Stuffing

STUFFING
1 stick butter
1 medium onion, chopped
1 celery stalk, chopped
1 cup mushrooms, chopped
2 cups chestnuts, roasted,
    peeled, chopped
2 tablespoons chopped parsley
4 cups bread crumbs
¼ teaspoon pepper
1 teaspoon salt
1 cup chicken stock
½ teaspoon thyme
1 teaspoon sage
½ teaspoon rosemary

TURKEY
1 stick butter
1 tablespoon Hungarian paprika
Salt and pepper
1 medium turkey (about 14 pounds)

In a skillet, melt 1 stick of butter, then sauté the onion, celery, and mushrooms for 10 minutes. Combine with the remaining ingredients. Set stuffing aside.

Preheat oven to 350° F. In a small saucepan, melt 1 stick of butter, then add the paprika and salt and pepper. Baste the turkey with this sauce.

Stuff the cavity of the turkey with the stuffing. Bake the stuffed turkey for 20 minutes per pound. Baste every ½ hour with the drippings. If necessary, cover the turkey with an oiled tea towel to prevent blackening on the top. (If there is any leftover stuffing, put it into a greased ovenproof dish, add a little water, and bake for 45 minutes next to the turkey.)

Mint Beef Stew with Chestnuts

4 tablespoons oil
2 ½ pounds tri-tip or
    other stew meat, diced
2 onions, chopped
6-ounce can tomato paste
1 cup red wine
5 cups water
2 tablespoons chopped mint
1 tablespoon oregano
1 bay leaf
¼ teaspoon pepper
½ teaspoon salt
4 ripe tomatoes, diced or stewed
4 zucchini, sliced
1 pound green beans, cut in half
1 ½ cups chestnuts, sliced
    (use toasted, fresh, or canned)

In a skillet or cast-iron casserole, heat the oil, then brown the meat and the onions. Stir in the tomato paste, red wine, water, and spices. Let the stew simmer for 1 ½ hours. Add the vegetables and chestnuts. Simmer for another 45 minutes.

If needed, add more water to the stew. Remove the bay leaf and serve hot with rice or boiled potatoes. Serves 6.

Shown opposite:
Mint Beef Stew with Chestnuts.

Hazelnut Meatballs

1 cup hazelnuts, ground
1 pound ground beef
1 pound ground pork
3 teaspoons salt
1 teaspoon pepper
½ teaspoon ginger
½ teaspoon nutmeg
1 teaspoon thyme
¼ cup flour
5 tablespoons cornstarch
¼ cup milk

Blend the hazelnuts with the beef, pork, spices, flour, and cornstarch. Then, little by little, beat in the milk until everything is well blended.

Make meatballs a little smaller than golf balls and, using a little oil, fry them over medium heat until they are thoroughly browned on all sides. Serve hot or cold. Makes 50 meatballs.

Hazelnuts

The hazelnut belongs to the same family as the filbert. In Norway, the hazelnut tree is dedicated to the god Thor. The Norwegian king's staff was made from hazelnut wood.

Hazelnuts have been eaten since the Stone Age. In ancient times, many people believed that a forked hazelnut twig had supernatural powers—it was used to find water and minerals underground.

Roasted Cornish Hens with Hazelnut Stuffing

STUFFING
1 ½ cups chicken broth
4 tablespoons butter, melted
1 small onion, chopped fine
¾ cup hazelnuts, chopped
4 teaspoons chopped parsley
2 cups or 4 slices dry bread, crusts
   removed and bread cut into slices
1 apple, peeled and chopped
1 ½ cups chopped spinach

HENS
4 Cornish game hens
4 tablespoons butter
1 ½ teaspoons red paprika
1 teaspoon salt
¾ teaspoon pepper
1 teaspoon thyme

In a pot, mix the chicken broth with all other stuffing ingredients. Simmer for 15 minutes.

Preheat oven to 375° F. Place the Cornish game hens in a roasting pan. Fill each with stuffing. Melt the butter, then blend in the spices. Spoon the butter and spice mixture over the hens. Roast for 1 hour and 10 minutes. Serves 8.

Veal with Lemon Butter and Hazelnut Crust

LEMON BUTTER
6 tablespoons butter, at room
  temperature
3 teaspoons lemon juice
2 teaspoons chopped parsley

VEAL
1 pound veal steaks
1 egg
4 tablespoons finely
  ground hazelnuts
4 tablespoons flour
1 teaspoon salt
¼ teaspoon pepper
Butter or oil for frying

Combine the butter, lemon juice, and
parsley and roll into a thick tube. Place
the tube in the freezer for 15 minutes.

Pound the veal steaks until tender.
Beat the egg slightly. Combine the
hazelnuts, flour, salt, and pepper. Dip
the veal steaks into the egg, then into the
flour mixture. Heat the butter or oil in a
skillet and over medium heat, fry the veal
until brown on both sides. Remove the
lemon butter from the freezer and cut
into slices. Serve the veal immediately
with the lemon butter on top. Serves 4.

Beef Peanut Teriyaki

2 pounds beef steak
  (tri-tip or sirloin)
1 cup teriyaki sauce
4 tablespoons peanut oil
1 tablespoon sesame seeds
½ teaspoon pepper
1 tablespoon peeled and finely
  chopped ginger root
1 cup raw peanuts
1 cup sliced zucchini
1 cup sliced celery in 2-inch strips
1 cup sliced red pepper
1 ½ cups long-grain rice, cooked
½ cup wild rice, cooked

Cut the beef into strips, then marinate
the strips in the teriyaki sauce for
2 hours. Heat the peanut oil and fry the
marinated beef in the oil until brown on
both sides. (Fry a few strips at a time and
set aside.) Combine all remaining
ingredients and stir-fry for 10 minutes.
Serve hot. Serves 6.

Peanut Chicken

1 large chicken
3 tablespoons peanut oil
1 large onion, chopped fine
1 cup raw peanuts, skinned
2 cups water
½ cup condensed coconut milk
2 carrots, peeled and sliced
3 celery stalks, chopped
1 green pepper, sliced thin
½ teaspoon crushed garlic
¼ teaspoon nutmeg
Salt and pepper to taste

Cut the meat from the chicken. Heat the oil and brown the chicken in it; set aside. Sauté the onion in a little oil for 6 minutes. Purée the peanuts and water in a food processor or blender; pour into a saucepan and simmer for 8 minutes, then stir in the coconut milk. Add the chicken, vegetables, garlic, nutmeg, and salt and pepper. Simmer for 45 minutes. Serve with rice. Serves 4.

Linguine with Pine Nut Pesto

This makes a light, yet satisfying meal when served with salad and bread.

2 cups basil fresh leaves
½ cup olive oil
3 tablespoons pine nuts,
    toasted (see page x)
5 garlic cloves, minced
1 teaspoon salt
1 teaspoon freshly ground pepper
5 tablespoons butter, melted or soft
½ cup Parmesan cheese, freshly grated
12-ounce package linguine

In a food processor or blender, combine all the ingredients except the cheese and the pasta, and blend until smooth. Add the cheese to the mixture and stir.

Fill a large pot with water and 1 teaspoon salt and bring to a boil. Add the linguine and boil for 12 minutes or as directed on package. Drain well, add the pesto, and serve immediately. Serves 4.

Shown opposite:
Linguine with Pine Nut Pesto.

Gyros with Piñon Nuts and Zadziky

ZADZIKY

1 ½ cups grated cucumber
2 cups sour cream or plain yogurt
½ teaspoon chopped mint
½ teaspoon ground or finely
   chopped garlic

GYROS

1 pound minute steaks
¼ cup piñon nuts, chopped fine
1 teaspoon oregano
¼ teaspoon allspice
¼ teaspoon cumin
½ teaspoon pepper
½ teaspoon salt
Oil for frying
2 tomatoes, chopped
1 onion, chopped fine
6 pita pockets

In a bowl, combine the cucumber and
the sour cream, then mix in the mint and
garlic. Chill. Cut the meat into strips.
Mix the piñon nuts with the oregano,
allspice, cumin, pepper, and salt. Coat
the steak strips with the nut mix, then
grill or fry the steaks until done on both
sides. Place the tomatoes and onion in
two small bowls. Cut the pitas in half
and warm in the oven. Fill the pockets
with the meat, tomatoes, onion, and
zadziky. Serve immediately. Serves 6.

Pine Nuts with Fettuccine Primavera

2 cups water
6 tablespoons butter
Salt and pepper
3 carrots, peeled and sliced
   into thin strips
1 ½ pounds sugar peas, strings removed
2 cups broccoli, cut into small bunches
1 ½ pounds fresh asparagus,
   cut into 3 pieces each
1 red pepper, cut into fine strips
4 yellow zucchini, cut into strips
4 tablespoons pine nuts
1 large yellow onion, peeled
   and cut into 8 pieces
12 ounces fettuccine noodles
6 tablespoons finely chopped parsley
1 cup freshly grated Parmesan cheese
4 tablespoons olive oil

Pour the water into a large pot. Add
3 tablespoons of the butter and pinches
of salt and pepper, the carrots, sugar peas,
broccoli, asparagus, red pepper, and zucchini. Bring to a boil and then let simmer
for 5 minutes. Remove the vegetables
from the water and place to the side. In a
frying pan, melt the remaining 3 tablespoons of butter and sauté the pine nuts
and onion for 5 minutes; set aside. Cook
the pasta according to package directions.
Strain the pasta and reheat the vegetables.
Combine the vegetables, pine nuts, parsley,
Parmesan cheese, and olive oil. Put the
pasta in a serving bowl and top with the
vegetables. Serve immediately. Serves 6.

Rice with Shrimp, Eggs, and Piñon Nuts

2 tablespoons olive oil
1 teaspoon chopped garlic
2 ½ cups long-grained rice
½ cup wild rice
1 onion, chopped
2 cups chicken broth
2 cups chopped asparagus,
    in 1-inch pieces
1 cup green peas
2 pounds shrimp,
    shelled and deveined
4 teaspoons lemon juice
¼ teaspoon thyme
¼ teaspoon pepper
4 teaspoons chopped parsley
½ cup piñon nuts
3 eggs
Soy sauce

In a skillet, heat the olive oil and sauté the garlic, rices, and onion for 8 minutes; add the chicken broth and simmer for 20 minutes. Stir in the vegetables, shrimp, lemon juice, and spices. Simmer until the shrimp is done (about 5 minutes). Toast the pine nuts in a dry frying pan for 5 minutes. In a small bowl, whisk the eggs together. Melt a little butter or oil in a skillet and pour in the eggs. Turn the heat down low and place a lid on the pan. Flip the eggs if necessary. When the eggs are set, cut the omelet into strips and mix with the rice. Stir all ingredients together. Serve immediately with soy sauce on the side. Serves 4.

Stuffed Salmon with Rice and Piñon Nuts

Serve this with wedges of lemon, boiled potatoes, and extra stuffing on the side.

1 ½ pounds salmon
3 teaspoons butter
½ cup finely chopped onions
½ teaspoon minced garlic
¾ cup piñon nuts
½ cup long-grain rice
2 cups water
1 teaspoon thyme
¼ teaspoon pepper
½ cup mushrooms, sliced
1 teaspoon dill

Preheat oven to 350° F. Rinse the fish inside and out, pat dry, and place on a large piece of greased foil. Melt the butter in a pan. Stir in the onions, garlic, piñon nuts, and rice and sauté for 6 minutes. Add the water, thyme, and pepper. Let the mixture simmer for 15 minutes. Add the mushrooms and dill. Stuff the cavity of the fish with the rice mixture and tie the fish together with cotton thread. Put the remaining stuffing in an ovenproof pot, add a little more water, and cover. Wrap the fish in foil and bake fish and extra stuffing for 45 minutes. Serves 8.

Pizzas with Pine Nuts, Shrimp, and Artichoke Hearts

PIZZA DOUGH
(or use frozen bread dough)
2 packages yeast
2 teaspoons sugar
1 cup warm water
½ cup whole wheat flour
3 cups all-purpose flour
1 teaspoon salt
4 tablespoons olive oil

SAUCE
4 tablespoons tomato paste
16-ounce can chopped tomatoes
4 teaspoons oregano
2 teaspoons sugar
½ teaspoon crushed garlic
Pinches of salt and pepper

TOPPING
1 cup small shrimp, peeled
8-ounce can artichoke hearts, sliced
1 cup pine nuts or walnuts
1 cup black olives, sliced
   (preferably not canned)
2 cups grated mozzarella cheese
1 cup grated Parmesan cheese

To make the pizza dough from scratch, stir the yeast, sugar, and warm water together, then let the dough sit for 5 minutes. Mix the flours and salt together, then add the yeast mixture and oil. Knead into a smooth dough. Place the dough in a bowl, cover with a tea towel, and set in a warm place. Let rise to double in size. In the meantime, prepare the sauce.

In a saucepan, combine all sauce ingredients. Over low heat, let the sauce simmer for 20 minutes.

After the dough has risen, preheat the oven to 375° F. Beat the dough down on a lightly floured board and cut it into four equal pieces. Roll each piece out to a thickness of ½ inch. Place the pizzas on a lightly floured cookie sheet or pizza pan. Bake for 12 minutes. Remove from the oven.

Spread the sauce evenly over the four pizzas. Top with the shrimp, artichoke hearts, pine nuts, and black olives. Sprinkle with the cheeses and bake for 40 more minutes. Serve hot. Serves 4.

Shown opposite:
Pizzas with Pine Nuts, Shrimp, and Artichoke Hearts.

Walnut Manicotti

This dish freezes well. In fact, the manicotti taste even better after being frozen, then thawed and heated thoroughly.

PASTA DOUGH
(or buy ready-made manicotti)
4 cups flour
5 eggs
3 tablespoons olive oil
3 tablespoons water

FILLING
4 cups ricotta cheese
4 cups grated mozzarella cheese
1 ½ cups grated Parmesan cheese
3 eggs
1 cup walnuts, chopped
4 tablespoons chopped parsley
¾ teaspoon nutmeg
¾ teaspoon salt
⅓ teaspoon pepper

SAUCE
18-ounce can whole tomatoes
1 medium onion, chopped fine
6 tablespoons tomato paste
2 teaspoons sugar
1 tablespoon oregano
½ teaspoon thyme
1 teaspoon crushed garlic
Pinch of cinnamon
½ cup red wine

TOPPING
1 ½ cups grated Parmesan cheese
2 tablespoons parsley

To make the pasta from scratch, combine flour, eggs, and oil. Knead into a dough and add water or another egg if the dough is too dry. Work the dough until smooth, then let it rest for 20 minutes before you cut it into slices. On a lightly floured board, roll out the dough (or use a pasta machine). Fold the dough in half, dust with flour, and roll it out again. Do this several times. The dough should finally be rolled out very thin. Cut the dough into rectangles that measure 10x15 inches. Place the pasta rectangles in a large pot of boiling salted water and boil for 2 minutes. Remove them from the water, rinse them with cold water, and lay them flat.

Combine all filling ingredients and stir until well blended. Spread the filling along one edge of the noodle and roll it into a tube. Place in a slightly greased ovenproof pan. Put as many as you will eat in the pan (the rest can be frozen). In a saucepan, combine all sauce ingredients together. Simmer for ½ hour, stirring occasionally.

Preheat oven to 375° F. Pour the sauce over the top of the manicotti and sprinkle with Parmesan cheese. Bake for 20 minutes. Just before serving, sprinkle parsley on top. Makes 24 manicotti.

Shown opposite: Walnut Manicotti.

Cabbage Rolls with Walnuts

1 medium cabbage
2 tablespoons vegetable oil
1 medium onion, chopped fine
¼ cup rice
1 pound ground beef
1 egg
½ cup walnuts, chopped
1 teaspoon salt
¼ teaspoon pepper
½ teaspoon thyme
¼ teaspoon rosemary, crushed

Steam the cabbage until the leaves can be easily removed. In the oil, sauté the onion and rice. In a bowl, combine all remaining ingredients, including the beef. Mix until well blended. Place 2 spoonfuls of this mixture onto a cabbage leaf, then roll and fold into a package. Continue until filling is used up. Place a few cabbage leaves in the bottom of a thick-bottomed saucepan, then layer the cabbage rolls tightly together on top of the leaves. Add enough water to cover the cabbage rolls, then add a pinch of salt to the water. Over low heat, let the cabbage rolls simmer for 1 hour. Remove from pan with a slotted spoon and serve. Serves 6.

Gnocchi with Walnut Pesto

PESTO
1 ½ cups basil leaves
2 teaspoons crushed garlic
1 cup walnuts
½ teaspoon salt
¼ cup grated Parmesan cheese
¼ cup olive oil
½ teaspoon pepper

GNOCCHI
4 tablespoons butter
2 ½ cups mashed potatoes
 (about 8 or 9 medium potatoes)
2 eggs
2 cups flour
Salt and pepper to taste
½ stick butter, melted
Grated Parmesan cheese

Blend all the pesto ingredients in a food processor or blender to make a thick paste.

Preheat oven to 350° F. Stir the butter into the potatoes. Put the potatoes on a lightly floured board and knead in the eggs and flour and salt and pepper. Fill a large pot with water and bring it to a boil. Form the dough into a long roll, about 3 inches in diameter, then cut the roll into ½-inch slices. Drop the slices into the boiling water. When the gnocchi rises to the surface, it is done. Place them on a baking sheet, brush with a little butter, and sprinkle with grated Parmesan cheese. Bake for 15 minutes. Serve hot with pesto sauce. Makes 20. Extra pesto can be stored in an airtight jar in the refrigerator and served hot or cold.

Four-Layer Pasta Pie

LAYER 1

4 cups cooked macaroni
¼ cup grated Parmesan cheese
3 eggs, slightly beaten
¼ cup half and half

LAYER 2

7 slices ham, cut into small strips

LAYER 3

2 cups ricotta cheese
10-ounce package frozen spinach,
    defrosted, drained and chopped
2 eggs
2 egg yolks
¼ cup grated mozzarella cheese
½ cup walnuts, chopped
¼ cup grated Parmesan cheese

LAYER 4

16-ounce can whole tomatoes
5 tablespoons tomato paste
½ cup water or red wine
1 teaspoon basil
½ teaspoon oregano
1 teaspoon crushed garlic
1 small onion, grated
1 teaspoon sugar
¼ teaspoon pepper
1 pinch of cinnamon
3 egg whites

Combine the layer 1 ingredients; pour into a 9-inch greased pie pan or spring-form pan. Layer the ham on top of the macaroni. Combine all ingredients for layer 3, then pour over the top of the ham. In a saucepan, combine all layer 4 ingredients except the egg whites. Simmer for 40 minutes, then cool.

Preheat oven to 375° F. Beat the egg whites until stiff, then fold into the tomato sauce. Pour this sauce over the ricotta cheese layer. Bake for 1 hour and 10 minutes. Remove from oven and let cool for 15 minutes before removing from the pan. Cut into wedges and serve. Serves 8.

Ham Pie with Walnuts

PIE CRUST
1 ½ cups flour
1 egg, beaten
1 ½ sticks butter

FILLING
3 eggs
1 cup milk
½ teaspoon salt
½ teaspoon pepper
2 cups boiled ham, cut into thin slices
1 cup broccoli, cut into small bunches
1 red pepper, sliced in thin slices
1 cup walnuts, chopped
2 cups grated cheddar cheese
1 onion, sliced in rings
¼ cup grated Parmesan cheese

Preheat oven to 350° F. Combine all pie crust ingredients and form a dough ball. Place the dough ball in a greased 9-inch pie pan. Using your fingers, press the dough out to evenly line the pie pan. Bake for 10 minutes.

In a bowl, beat the 3 eggs, milk, salt, and pepper. Stir in the ham, broccoli, red pepper, nuts, and cheddar cheese. Pour the mixture into the pie crust, spread the onion rings on top, sprinkle with Parmesan cheese, and bake for 30 minutes. Serve hot or cold. Serves 6.

Lamb with Walnut Pesto

For an outstanding meal, serve this with new potatoes, glazed carrots, and steamed asparagus.

PESTO
½ cup walnuts
4 garlic cloves, cut into halves
2 cups fresh mint leaves
1 cup fresh basil
⅓ cup olive oil
2 tablespoons lemon juice

LAMB
6-pound leg of lamb
3 garlic cloves, sliced into thirds
Salt and pepper to taste

In a blender or food processor, blend all pesto ingredients until smooth.

Place the leg of lamb in a roasting pan. Cut nine small pockets in the lamb and insert a piece of garlic in each. Spread the pesto sauce over the lamb and cover tightly with foil or plastic; chill overnight.

Preheat oven to 350° F. Remove the wrapping, then roast the lamb for approximately 2 hours. Slice the meat thin. Serves 6–8.

Chicken Breasts with Walnuts and Artichoke Hearts

3 tablespoons olive oil
1 cup mushrooms, sliced
¼ cup diced onion
½ teaspoon chopped fresh garlic
½ cup artichoke hearts, sliced
¼ cup walnuts, chopped
¼ tablespoon oregano
1 tablespoon basil
¼ teaspoon pepper
½ teaspoon salt
¾ cup grated mozzarella
4 chicken breasts, boneless and skinless
1 egg, beaten
½ cup dry bread crumbs
1 teaspoon paprika

Preheat oven to 350° F. Sauté mushrooms, onions, and garlic in the olive oil. Add artichoke hearts, walnuts, and spices. Stir over low heat for 2 minutes. Remove pan from heat, add mozzarella cheese, and blend all together. Spread 2 spoonfuls of the mixture on each chicken breast, roll up each breast, and place in a greased baking pan, seam side down. Brush the breasts with the beaten egg and sprinkle the bread crumbs and paprika over the top. Bake for 15 minutes. Cut the breast into slices approximately ¼-inch thick and arrange on plates. Serves 4.

Roasted Chicken with Honey Glaze and Walnut Stuffing

STUFFING
2 teaspoons vegetable oil
½ onion, chopped
5 mushrooms, chopped
1 cup chicken broth
½ cup chopped celery
½ cup chopped walnuts
2 tablespoons bulgur wheat
Salt and pepper
½ teaspoon sage

CHICKEN
1 large roasting chicken, rinsed
    inside and out
1 tablespoon butter
¼ cup honey
1 teaspoon Dijon mustard
1 tablespoon white wine or water
¼ teaspoon coriander
⅛ teaspoon pepper

In a pan, heat the oil and sauté the onions and mushrooms until the onions are clear. Add the chicken broth and all other stuffing ingredients to the onions and mushrooms. Let the mixture simmer for 5 minutes. Fill the chicken with the stuffing and place it in a roasting pan.

Preheat oven to 350° F. In a pot, melt the butter; remove from heat. Add the honey and mustard and blend well. Stir in the wine, coriander and pepper. Pour the glaze over the entire chicken. Bake for 1 hour and 45 minutes. Remove stuffing from chicken. Serves 6.

Spinach, Cheese, and Walnut Pies

2 teaspoons olive oil
½ pound feta cheese, crumbled
1 bunch spinach leaves, rinsed and
    chopped, or 10-ounce package
    frozen chopped spinach, defrosted
    and drained
½ cup walnuts, chopped
1 cup black Greek olives, pitted
    and halved
¼ teaspoon mint
¼ teaspoon thyme
¼ teaspoon oregano
¼ teaspoon pepper
8 sheets phyllo dough
½ cup butter, melted

Preheat oven to 350° F. In a bowl,
combine all ingredients except the dough
and the melted butter. Cut each sheet of
phyllo dough into four squares. Brush a
square on one side with the butter. Then
place a heaping spoonful of stuffing in
the center of the buttered side. Fold the
square into a package. Take a second
square, brush it with butter, and wrap it
around the package as a second layer.
Place all of the packages on a greased
baking tray. Brush each with butter, then
bake for 20 minutes or until golden
brown on top. Makes 16.

Swordfish in Cold Garlic Sauce

SWORDFISH
4 tablespoons butter
2 pounds swordfish,
    or 4 swordfish steaks
2 tablespoons lemon juice
Salt and pepper

GARLIC SAUCE
4 slices white bread, crusts removed
2 teaspoons finely chopped garlic
2 tablespoons cider vinegar
¼ cup walnuts
6 tablespoons olive oil

Soak the bread in water for 3 minutes;
then squeeze the water out. In a food
processor or blender, blend the bread,
garlic, vinegar, and nuts until smooth.
Add the oil, a little at a time, until it
is all used. (This sauce can also be
served as an appetizer with carrot and
celery sticks.)
   In a frying pan, melt the butter, then fry
the fish on both sides for 4 minutes or
until done (the bone will be loose).
Sprinkle with lemon juice and salt and
pepper. Spoon the garlic sauce over the
fish, then serve. Serves 4

Shown opposite:
Stir-Fried Shrimp with Water Chestnuts, page 62.

Walnut-Stuffed Beef Filet

2-pound filet of beef,
  tri-tip or filet mignon
½ onion
8 mushrooms
½ cup walnuts
1 teaspoon chopped fresh basil
6 teaspoons chopped parsley
1 apple, peeled and cut into
  small pieces
Salt and pepper

Preheat oven to 350° F. Using the handle
of a wooden spoon, punch a hole in the
middle of the filet or slice the meat
lengthwise, without puncturing the meat
all the way through. Chop the onion,
mushrooms, and walnuts and mix with
the basil and parsley. Stir in the apple
pieces, and then fill the pocket of the filet
with the stuffing. Sprinkle salt and
pepper over the meat. If using tri-tip, roll
the stuffed meat up and tie it with cotton
string. Place the filet in an ungreased
baking pan, and bake for
1 ½ hours. Serves 6.

Stir-Fried Shrimp with Water Chestnuts

2 tablespoons olive oil
2 tablespoons finely
  chopped fresh ginger
1 pound shrimp, shelled
4 tablespoons cooking sherry
1 yellow pepper, cut into thin strips
1 pound snow peas
1 cup canned water chestnuts
2 tablespoons soy sauce
1 tablespoon cornstarch

In a skillet, heat the oil and the ginger
over low heat for 5 minutes. Add the
shrimp and sherry. Simmer until the
shrimp are done (about 7 minutes).
Add the pepper, snow peas, and water
chestnuts. Stir for 2 minutes. In a small
bowl, blend the soy sauce and cornstarch.
Pour this over the shrimp and vegetables.
Bring to a boil and then remove from the
heat. Serve hot over rice. Serves 4.

Water Chestnuts

The Chinese water chestnut is a
grasslike plant that grows
underwater in streams and lakes.
The white flesh can be eaten raw,
slightly boiled, broiled, or pickled.
Native to China, it is widely used in
Chinese food.

The water chestnut was
introduced to the United States in
1934 and now can be found
growing on the Atlantic coast. It also
grows in subtropical places like Asia
and Africa.

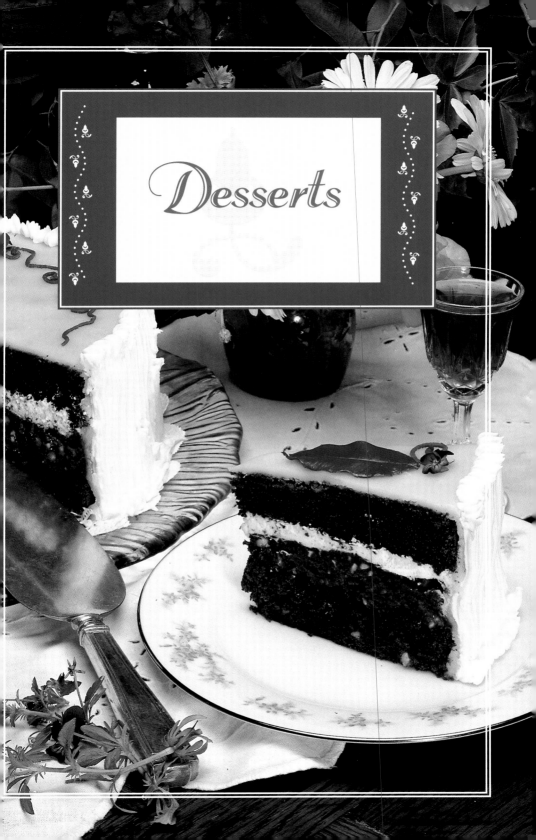

Desserts

Almond and Strawberry Cheesecake

CHEESECAKE
2 cups crumbled graham crackers
4 tablespoons butter, melted
1 teaspoon almond extract
1 cup almonds, ground
1 ½ cups sugar
16 ounces cream cheese
1 cup sour cream
3 tablespoons cornstarch
5 eggs
1 ½ cups strawberries, hulled

TOPPING
1 pint whipping cream
3 tablespoons sugar

DECORATION
2 cups sliced strawberries
¼ cup sliced almonds, toasted

Preheat oven to 350° F. Place the graham crackers in a 9-inch greased cake pan. Mix the melted butter with the almond extract and drip this over the graham crackers. Blend together the almonds, ½ cup sugar, cream cheese, sour cream, cornstarch, eggs, and strawberries. Pour the strawberry batter over the graham crackers. Place the cake pan in a larger pan filled with water. Bake for 1 ½ hours. Let the cake chill for few hours or overnight.

Whip together the cream and 3 tablespoons sugar until peaks form. Decorate the chilled cheesecake with whipped cream and sliced strawberries. Press the toasted almonds into the sides of the cheesecake. Serves 12.

Almond, Apple, and Apricot Pie

PIE CRUST
1 stick butter or vegetable
  shortening, at room temperature
1 ½ cups flour
½ cup almonds, ground
1 tablespoon water

FILLING
4 apples, peeled and sliced thin
20 fresh apricots, cut in half,
  stems and pits removed
½ cup water
2 tablespoons cornstarch
4 tablespoons honey
1 cup slivered almonds

TOPPING
Whipped cream or vanilla ice cream

Preheat oven to 350° F. Combine all pie crust ingredients and form a dough ball. Place the dough ball in a greased 9-inch pie pan. Using your fingers, press the dough out to evenly line the pie pan.

Layer the apples in the pie pan, then place the apricots on top, round side up. Stir the water, cornstarch, and honey together, and pour over the apricots. Sprinkle the slivered almonds on top. Bake the pie for 45 minutes. Top with whipped cream or ice cream. Serves 8.

Shown previous page:
Hazelnut Truffle Chocolate Cake, page 86.

Shown opposite: Almond and Strawberry Cheesecake.

Almond Apple Pie

DOUGH
3 ½ cups flour
½ pound or 1 stick butter
¼ cup vegetable shortening
2 eggs
4 tablespoons cold water

FILLING
2 cups chunky applesauce
6 apples, peeled and sliced
½ cup raisins
1 cup slivered almonds
5 tablespoons lemon juice
1 teaspoon ginger
¼ cup brown sugar
¼ cup sugar
3 tablespoons butter, melted

Preheat oven to 350° F. In a bowl, combine the flour, butter, and shortening; add the eggs and cold water. Roll half of the pie dough out and place it in a lightly greased and floured 9-inch pie pan. Layer the pie first with the applesauce, then with the apple slices. Sprinkle the raisins and almonds on top. Combine the lemon juice, ginger, sugars, and melted butter and pour over the top. Roll out the remaining dough and cut it into strips. Weave the strips into a top for the pie. Bake for 40 minutes or until the crust is golden brown. Serves 9–12.

Almond Bread Pudding with Raspberry Sauce

PUDDING
5 slices dry white bread
2 cups cookie or cake crumbs
½ cup butter
1 cup hot milk
2 teaspoons vanilla
Grated rind and juice of 1 orange
1 cup almonds, chopped fine
5 eggs

RASPBERRY SAUCE
2 cups raspberries, fresh or frozen
½ cup water
1 teaspoon cornstarch

Preheat oven to 350° F. Cut the crusts off the bread and cut the bread into cubes. Mix the bread and cookie or cake crumbs. Melt the butter in the milk, add the vanilla and pour this mixture over the bread and cake crumbs. Let sit for 10 minutes. Stir in the grated orange rind, the orange juice, and the finely chopped almonds and mix well. Separate the egg whites from the egg yolks. Blend the egg yolks into the bread mixture. In a separate bowl, beat the egg whites stiff. Fold the whites carefully into the pudding. Pour the pudding into a pudding mold and cover with foil. Place the mold inside a larger pot or mold and fill the outside pot with water. Place in the oven and bake for 1 hour.

Meanwhile, put the raspberries in a saucepan. Mix the water and cornstarch. Add to the raspberries and bring the mixture to a slow boil. Simmer for 10 minutes, stirring occasionally. Serve hot or cold over the pudding. Serves 6.

Almond Brick Cake with Chocolate Cream

CAKE
5 eggs
1 ½ cups sugar
1 ¼ cups flour
1 cup almonds, ground
1 teaspoon baking powder

CHOCOLATE FILLING
2 sticks butter
2 cups powdered sugar
2 egg yolks
2 tablespoons cocoa powder
2 teaspoons vanilla
¼ cup maraschino cherries, chopped

Preheat oven to 350° F. Beat the eggs and sugar together until thick and fluffy. In a separate bowl, combine the flour, almonds, and baking powder. Carefully fold this mixture into the eggs and sugar. Line a cookie sheet with waxed paper or greased foil. Bake the cake for 15 minutes on the cookie sheet. While the cake is baking, spread out a tea towel on your work space and sprinkle it with a little sugar. When the cake is done, turn it upside down onto the tea towel, remove the waxed paper or foil from the bottom immediately, and let the cake cool in that position.

To make the filling, beat butter and powdered sugar together; add the egg yolks, cocoa powder, and vanilla. Cut the cake into three equal layers. Spread half of the chocolate filling on one layer. Sprinkle with half of the cherries. Place a second layer of cake on top, and spread the rest of the chocolate over it. Cover with the remaining cherries. Place the last layer on top. Chill before serving. Serves 10.

Almond Cake with Chocolate and Cream

CAKE
¾ cup butter
1 cup sugar
4 eggs
1 teaspoon almond extract
2 cups almonds, blanched and ground
1 ½ cups powdered sugar
½ cup sour cream
1 ½ cups flour
1 ½ teaspoons baking powder

FROSTING
1 cup sweet or semi-sweet chocolate
1 tablespoon butter or margarine
2 tablespoons water
8 tablespoons powdered sugar
½ pint whipping cream
2 tablespoons powdered sugar

Preheat oven to 350° F. In a large bowl, beat the butter and sugar until fluffy. Add 1 egg at a time. Beat well, then add the almond extract. Mix the ground almonds and powdered sugar; add to the batter and beat. Stir in the sour cream. Sift in the flour and baking powder and beat until well blended. Pour the cake batter into a 9-inch greased and floured springform pan. Bake in the oven for 50 minutes or until a fork comes out clean. Let the cake cool completely before removing it from the pan.

To make the frosting, melt the chocolate with the butter, water, and 8 tablespoons powdered sugar and stir until lump free; spread it over the cake. Whip the cream with the 2 tablespoons powdered sugar until stiff. Decorate with the whipped cream when the chocolate frosting is completely cool. Serves 10 – 12.

Almond Caramel Ice Cream

1 ½ cups brown sugar
½ cup water
1 teaspoon vanilla
1 cup whipping cream
4 tablespoons butter
1 ½ cups almonds, chopped
½ gallon vanilla ice cream

In a saucepan, combine the brown sugar, water, and vanilla. Simmer for 10 minutes while stirring gently. Slowly stir in the cream and butter and continue stirring until well blended. Take the ice cream out of the freezer to soften. Add the nuts to the saucepan and stir for 5 minutes. Pour the mixture onto a greased aluminum sheet and let it cool. Cut the mixture into small pieces and quickly stir them into the ice cream. Pour the ice cream into a mold and refrigerate for 30 minutes. Pop out of the mold and serve. Serves 6.

Almond-Filled Cookies

COOKIES
2 ½ cups flour
4 tablespoons sugar
1 teaspoon grated orange rind
1 egg
1 cup butter or vegetable shortening
2 tablespoons water

FILLING
½ cup almonds, blanched and
   chopped fine
8-ounce package cream cheese
¾ cup powdered sugar
1 egg white
1 teaspoon almond extract
1 teaspoon grated orange rind

In a bowl, mix the flour, sugar, and orange rind. Blend in the egg and butter, then add the water and blend. Knead until a dough is formed, then cover and place in the refrigerator for 1 hour or more.

Preheat oven to 350° F. On a cookie sheet, spread the almonds. Bake for 10 minutes. Beat the cream cheese with the powdered sugar and egg white. Add the almond extract and the orange rind. Stir in the toasted almonds.

On a lightly floured board, form the dough into a long log. Using a rolling pin, roll the dough out to a thickness of ¼ inch. Spread the filling down the middle of the length of the dough. Roll the dough back into a log, and cut the log into 30 cookies. Place the cookies on a greased cookie sheet, flat side down. Bake for 15 minutes. Makes 30 cookies.

Almond Fruit Cake

This cake tastes best if tightly wrapped in foil and stored in a cool place for three days before frosting and eating.

CAKE
2 sticks butter
2 cups brown sugar
5 eggs
2 ½ cups flour
2 teaspoons baking powder
Grated rind of 2 oranges
Grated rind of ½ lemon
1 cup raisins
1 cup maraschino cherries, chopped
¼ teaspoon cardamom
1 ½ cups whole almonds, blanched

FROSTING
3 cups powdered sugar
¼ cup orange juice

Preheat oven to 400° F. Beat the butter and sugar together until fluffy. Beat in the eggs, one at a time. Sift in the flour and baking powder. Then add the grated orange and lemon rinds and the rest of the cake ingredients except the almonds. Pour the batter into a 9-inch, greased and floured cake pan or two loaf pans. Sprinkle the almonds on top of the un-baked batter, then bake for 45 minutes or until a fork comes out clean.

To make the frosting, stir the ingredients together until smooth. Spread over the cake and decorate with extra maraschino cherries. Serves 12.

Almond Hats

This cookie dough can also be used to make other cookie shapes with different fillings.

DOUGH
1 ½ sticks butter
2 cups flour
1 ½ tablespoons sugar
1 egg yolk
1 whole egg

FILLING
2 cups almonds, blanched and ground
2 cups powdered sugar
2 egg whites

GLAZE
1 ½ cups powdered sugar
½ egg white

In a bowl, cut the butter into the flour and sugar, then add the egg yolk and whole egg. Quickly work the dough into a ball. Leave in the bowl, cover, and chill in the refrigerator for 1 hour.

Preheat the oven to 350° F. Combine the almonds with the 2 cups powdered sugar and 2 egg whites. Work the mix-ture until smooth. Roll the chilled dough out flat onto a lightly floured board. With a round cookie cutter, cut circles out of the dough. Place a teaspoon of almond filling in the middle of each, then fold three sides of the dough in and pinch the edges together. Place the cookies on a greased cookie sheet. Bake for 12 minutes.

Stir the 1 ½ cups powdered sugar and ½ egg white together. Let the cookies cool completely and brush with the glaze. Makes 24 cookies.

Almond Ice Cream Cake

CAKE
2 cups flour
2 teaspoons grated lemon rind
¾ cup almonds, ground fine
1 egg white
1 ¾ teaspoons cream of tartar
2 cups sugar
½ teaspoon salt
1 teaspoon almond extract
4 teaspoons lemon juice

TOPPING
1 ½ cups slivered almonds
½ cup powdered sugar

FILLING
1 pint vanilla ice cream
1 ½ pints raspberries

CHOCOLATE SAUCE
1 ½ cups semi-sweet chocolate
1 cup powdered sugar
2 tablespoons butter

Preheat oven to 375° F. In a bowl, combine the flour, lemon rind, and ground almonds. In a clean, dry bowl, beat the egg white with the cream of tartar until stiff; add the sugar and salt, a little at a time, while beating. Stir in the almond extract and lemon juice. Fold the flour mixture into the egg white carefully and pour the batter into a 9-inch spring-form pan. Sprinkle the slivered almonds and ½ cup powdered sugar on top. Bake the cake for 45 minutes or until a skewer comes out clean. Let the cake cool.

In a bowl, combine the ice cream and raspberries and quickly beat until blended. Cut the cake in two layers. Spread ice cream between the two layers and freeze for 45 minutes.

In the meantime, make the chocolate sauce. In a double boiler, combine all ingredients and melt over medium heat. Then let it cool, and pour this sauce over the top of the cake just before serving. Serves 12.

Apple Cake with Almond Topping

CAKE
¾ cup butter
1 ½ cups sugar
1 cup sour cream
1 teaspoon vanilla
5 eggs
2 ½ cups flour
2 teaspoons baking powder
6 apples, peeled and cut into thin slices

ALMOND FROSTING
½ cup butter
1 cup honey
3 tablespoons flour
½ cup water
2 cups slivered almonds

Preheat the oven to 350° F. Beat the butter and sugar together until light and fluffy. Add the sour cream, vanilla, and eggs and mix well. Sift in the flour and baking powder, stirring until well blended. Grease a 12-inch baking pan and fill it with three-quarters of the batter. Layer the apples on top and pour the remaining batter over them. Bake the cake for 30 minutes.

Make the frosting in the meantime. In a saucepan, melt the butter. Add the honey, flour, and water and blend until smooth. Add the slivered almonds and stir over low heat for 5 minutes. When the cake has baked for ½ hour, remove it from the oven and spread the frosting over the top. Then return it to the oven for another 15 – 20 minutes or until a fork comes out clean. Serves 12.

Apple Dessert with Almonds

This is a traditional Sunday dessert in Norway.

½ cup water
8 apples, peeled and cut into small chunks
8 tablespoons sugar
1 ½ sticks butter
4 cups bread crumbs
2 cups almonds, chopped

Preheat oven to 350° F. In a saucepan, combine the water, apples, and 4 tablespoons of the sugar. Cook until the apples are soft. With a fork, mash the apples. In a skillet, stir together the remaining 4 tablespoons of sugar, the butter, and the bread crumbs and heat, continuing to stir, until slightly brown. Pour half of the bread crumb mixture into a greased ovenproof dish. Spoon the apples on top. Mix the nuts with the remaining bread crumb mixture and then spread it over the apples. Bake for 20 minutes. Serve warm topped with whipped cream or vanilla ice cream. Serves 6.

Chocolate-Dipped Almond Cookies

COOKIES
1 ¼ cups butter, soft
½ cup sugar
2 cups powdered sugar
2 teaspoons almond extract
2 eggs
1 cup almonds, ground fine
3 cups flour
1 ½ teaspoons cream of tartar
1 teaspoon baking powder

FROSTING
1 cup sweet or semi-sweet chocolate
2 tablespoons water
1 tablespoon butter

Preheat oven to 375° F. Beat the butter and sugars together until creamy and fluffy. Add the almond extract; blend well. Add the remaining ingredients and mix. On a lightly floured board, form the cookie dough into a long roll. Cut the roll into approximately 40 1-inch slices. Press each slice into a flat circle, then place the cookies on a greased cookie sheet. Bake for 15 minutes.

In a double boiler, combine the frosting ingredients and melt over low heat. Let the cookies cool completely, then dip half of each cookie into the melted chocolate. Makes 40 cookies.

Shown opposite: Chocolate-Dipped Almond Cookies and Danish Almond Macaroons, this page; and Pistachio Chocolate Truffles, page 92.

Danish Almond Macaroons

3 cups shredded coconut
1 ½ cups chopped or slivered
   almonds, blanched
1 cup sugar
⅓ cup flour
¼ teaspoon salt
5 egg whites
1 teaspoon almond extract
30 maraschino cherries for garnish

Preheat oven to 350° F. In a bowl, mix all dry ingredients. In a separate bowl, use a fork to beat the egg whites with the almond extract. Beat for 3 minutes. Add this mixture to the dry ingredients and stir until well blended. Drop dough by the spoonful onto a greased cookie sheet. Garnish each with a cherry. Bake for 25 minutes or until edges are slightly brown. Remove cookies from pan before completely cool; if they are removed while hot, they will fall apart, and if they have cooled too much, they will stick to the pan. Cool the macaroons completely before storing in a closed container. Makes 30 macaroons.

Fried Bananas with Almonds

These taste great with vanilla ice cream.

4 bananas, not too ripe
4 tablespoons flour
4 teaspoons butter
4 teaspoons orange marmalade
4 teaspoons lemon juice
1 teaspoon grated lemon peel
3 teaspoons finely chopped almonds
½ cup rum or cognac

Peel the bananas and cut them lengthwise, then sprinkle them with flour. Melt the butter in a frying pan, and fry the bananas on each side for 5 minutes. In a bowl, mix the marmalade with the lemon juice, grated lemon peel, and chopped almonds. Pour this mixture over the bananas and fry for 2 more minutes. Just before removing from the pan, pour the rum or cognac over the bananas and light it. Serve flaming. Serves 4.

Fruit Bars with Almonds

1 ½ cups dried apricots
1 cup dried apples
1 cup dried prunes
1 ½ cups water
1 teaspoon vanilla
2 cups flour
2 cups old-fashioned oats
1 cup brown sugar or honey
1 cup butter, melted
1 egg
1 ½ cups almonds

Soak the apricots, apples, and prunes in water for 2 hours; drain. In a blender, purée the fruit with 1 ½ cups water and the vanilla, then pour into a pot and simmer on low heat for 15 minutes. Add more water if needed.

Preheat oven to 350° F. Line a baking pan with slightly greased waxed paper or aluminum foil. Combine the flour, oats, brown sugar, butter, and egg and mix well. Using your hands, press half of this mixture into the bottom of the baking pan and bake for 15 minutes. Remove from the oven and spread the fruit mixture over the baked portion. Cover the fruit with the remaining flour mixture. Press the nuts into the dough on top. Bake for 30 minutes. Let cool before cutting into squares. Makes 24 fruit bars.

Fruit Salad with Toasted Almonds and Ice Cream

1 pint strawberries, halved or whole
1 cup seedless grapes, halved
11-ounce can mandarin oranges
3 cups honeydew melon balls
2 bananas, peeled and sliced
¼ cup orange liqueur
½ cup water
2 cups vanilla ice cream
1 ½ cups sliced almonds

Preheat oven to 350° F. Spread the almonds on a cookie sheet and toast in the oven for 10 minutes.

Carefully mix the fruit and place it in six glasses. In a small bowl, stir the liqueur and water together and pour over the fruit. Chill for ½ hour. Just before serving, add a large scoop of ice cream to each glass and sprinkle with almonds. Serves 6.

Honey Nut Cake

4 eggs
1 cup sugar
½ cup butter or margarine, melted
1 cup honey
2 teaspoons baking powder
3 cups flour
1 ½ cups almonds, chopped
½ teaspoon ginger
1 teaspoon cloves
¼ teaspoon cinnamon
24 whole almonds, blanched,
    for decoration

Preheat oven to 350° F. Beat together the eggs, sugar, and butter. Warm the honey, then stir it into the batter. Add the baking powder, flour, chopped almonds, and spices. Blend well. Pour the batter into a 9-inch greased and floured baking pan. Place the whole almonds on top. Bake for 1 hour and 10 minutes, or until a fork inserted in the cake comes out clean. Serves 12.

Pear Pie with Almond Crust

CRUST

3 cups flour
2 teaspoons sugar
1 cup almonds, ground
1 egg
½ pound butter, at room temperature

FILLING

10 fresh pears
3 teaspoons sugar
3 teaspoons lemon juice
1 cup almonds, ground

TOPPING

½ pint whipping cream
2 tablespoons sugar

In a bowl, blend the flour, 2 teaspoons sugar, and 1 cup ground almonds. Beat the egg slightly and mix it in. Add the butter, then knead the dough until it is a smooth form. Using half of the dough and some flour, roll the dough out until it is ¼-inch thick. Line the pie form and cut off the excess dough.

Preheat oven to 375° F. Peel and core the pears and cut them into round slices. Place the slices into a pot, sprinkle with 3 teaspoons sugar, and add the lemon juice. Fill the pot with water until it covers the pears. Bring to a slow boil, then simmer for 5 minutes. Remove the pears from the pot with a slotted spoon and place them in the pie shell. Sprinkle the 1 cup ground almonds on top.

Cut the remaining dough in strips. Criss-cross the strips over the top of the pie. Bake for 45 minutes or until golden brown.

Whip the cream and 2 tablespoons sugar together until stiff. Top the pie with the whipped cream and serve. Serves 8.

Sandcakes with Raspberry Cream

SANDCAKES

2 eggs
1 ¾ cups sugar
8 ounces or 1 ½ cups almonds, ground
½ teaspoon almond extract
4 cups flour
2 ½ sticks butter

FILLING

½ cup water
1 envelope gelatin
2 cups fresh raspberries, mashed
   (or use frozen raspberries, defrosted
   and drained)
1 pint whipping cream
4 tablespoons sugar
50 whole fresh raspberries for
   decoration, if available

Preheat the oven to 350° F. Beat the eggs and 1 ¾ cups sugar until stiff. Add the almonds, almond extract and flour, and mix well. Add the butter, then knead the ingredients into a dough. Roll the dough into a long tube and slice it into 50 small pieces. Press each piece into a greased sandcake form or muffin tin until the form is completely covered with a thin layer of dough. Bake for 10 minutes or until the cakes are crisp and golden in color. Let the cakes cool before removing them from the forms.

Meanwhile, boil the water and stir in the gelatin. Place the mashed raspberries in a bowl and stir in the gelatin mixture. Set aside to cool. Whip the cream and 4 tablespoons sugar until stiff. Fold into the raspberry mixture. Fill the sandcakes with the raspberry mixture. Decorate with the whole raspberries. Chill for 1 hour before serving. Makes 50 cakes.

Double-Chocolate Brazil Nut Brownies

8 ounces unsweetened chocolate
2 ½ sticks butter
3 cups sugar
3 teaspoons vanilla
6 eggs
1 ¾ cups flour
2 cups chopped Brazil nuts, or
   1 cup chopped walnuts and
   1 cup chopped almonds
1 cup white chocolate chips

Preheat oven to 350° F. In a double boiler, melt the chocolate with the butter, sugar, and vanilla over medium heat. Let cool a little, then beat in the eggs, flour, and nuts. Pour the batter into a 9x13-inch pan and bake for 30 minutes. Makes 24 brownies.

Brazil Nuts

Another name for the Brazil nut is para nut. These nuts are grown not only in Brazil, but also in Venezuela, Chile, and Africa. Brazil nut trees grow very tall—up to 150 feet. Usually, 12 to 24 kernels are clustered together, making the fruit the size of a man's head, weighing two to four pounds. The nuts are best to buy between November and February.

Coconut Cake

CAKE
½ cup butter, soft
1 cup sugar
3 eggs
1 cup sour cream
1 ½ teaspoons vanilla
1 ½ cups flour
¼ cup wheat germ
1 ½ cups shredded coconut
2 teaspoons baking powder
1 teaspoon cinnamon
½ teaspoon nutmeg

FROSTING
2 cups powdered sugar
½ cup shredded coconut
1 teaspoon lemon juice

Preheat oven to 350° F. In a bowl, beat together the butter and sugar, then add the eggs, one at a time. Beat in the sour cream, vanilla, flour, wheat germ, coconut, baking powder, and spices. Blend well and pour the batter into a 9-inch springform pan. Bake for 40 minutes or until a fork comes out clean.

To make the frosting, combine all ingredients and stir until lump free. Spread over the cooled cake. Serves 12.

Shown opposite:
Sandcakes with Raspberry Cream,
page 77.

Coconut Drops

4 egg whites
2 cups brown sugar
4 cups cornflakes
1 ½ cups walnuts, chopped
2 cups shredded coconut
2 teaspoons vanilla

Preheat oven to 350° F. Beat the egg whites until stiff, then beat in the brown sugar. Blend in all other ingredients. Using a spoon, drop the dough onto a greased cookie sheet. Bake for 20 minutes. Remove the coconut drops from the cookie sheet immediately so they don't stick. Makes 30 cookies.

Coconut

The coconut palm grows best near the sea, reaches 100 feet in height, and is originally from India. Its fruit is a staple of the West African diet. Fresh coconuts contain a lot of water. The white meat found inside is used grated. Coconut oil is used in cosmetics, margarine, and soup. Grated coconut is used in sweet desserts, rice, and curry dishes.

Sunshine Coconut Cookies

These cookies taste especially nice with tea.

2 cups flour
2 sticks butter
1 cup powdered sugar
2 cups sugar
5 eggs
2 teaspoons baking powder
2 cups shredded carrots
1 ½ cups shredded coconut
½ cup fresh orange juice

Preheat oven to 350° F. In a bowl, combine the flour, butter, and powdered sugar. Press into a 12-inch baking pan and bake for 15 minutes. Beat the sugar and eggs until stiff. Add the baking powder, then stir in the carrots, coconut, and orange juice; blend well. Spread this over the baked bottom layer. Bake for 45 more minutes. Let the cake cool before cutting into small squares. Makes 25 cookies.

Banana Pie with Hazelnut Topping

DOUGH
1 ½ cups flour
2 teaspoons sugar
1 egg
¼ pound butter, at room temperature

FILLING
2 cups milk
3 tablespoons cornstarch
1 cup sugar
1 ½ teaspoons vanilla
4 egg yolks, beaten
½ cup heavy cream
4 bananas
Juice of ½ lemon

NUT TOPPING
½ cup sugar
1 cup water
¾ cup hazelnuts, chopped

Preheat oven to 350° F. In a bowl, mix the flour and 2 teaspoons sugar with the egg. Knead in the butter and form a dough ball. Place the dough ball in a greased 9-inch pie pan. Using your thumbs (or fingers), press this pie dough out to evenly line the pie pan. Prick holes in the dough with a fork and bake for 15 minutes. Let cool.

In a thick-bottomed saucepan, combine the milk, cornstarch, 1 cup sugar, and vanilla. Bring this to a slow boil, stirring continuously, then beat in the egg yolks and cream. While stirring, let the mixture simmer until it is thick. Remove from the heat and let cool. Slice the bananas and dip each slice into the lemon juice. Layer the sliced bananas on top of the pie crust and pour the custard mixture over them.

In a skillet or saucepan, combine the ½ cup sugar and water. Stirring occasionally, simmer for about 10 minutes. When the mixture has turned light brown, stir in the chopped hazelnuts. Remove from the heat and cool slightly. Pour the mixture on top of the pie. Chill the pie before serving. Serves 8.

Cream Cheese Ice Cream with Strawberries and Hazelnuts

16 ounces cream cheese
3 cups powdered sugar
3 egg yolks
2 tablespoons lemon juice
2 cups strawberries, mashed
1 pint heavy cream
½ cup hazelnuts, chopped

In a bowl, beat the cream cheese and powdered sugar together until light and fluffy. Add the egg yolks and lemon juice. Mix well and stir in the strawberries. In a separate bowl, beat the cream until stiff peaks form. Gently fold the cream into the cream cheese mixture. Pour into an airtight container and store in the freezer overnight. Remove the cream cheese mixture 20 minutes before serving in order to let it thaw slightly. Sprinkle the hazelnuts on top, garnish with a few whole strawberries, and serve. Serves 8.

Chocolate-Filled Hazelnut Cookies

A definite hit with the kids!

DOUGH
2 ½ cups or 8 ounces finely
    ground almonds, firmly packed
3 cups powdered sugar
3 egg whites

FILLING
2 tablespoons butter
1 cup semi-sweet chocolate chips
¼ cup hazelnuts, ground
¼ cup powdered sugar
1 teaspoon vanilla

FROSTING
½ cup powdered sugar
A few drops of lemon juice

Combine ground almonds and 3 cups powdered sugar. Stir in the egg whites, a little at a time. Work the dough until it is smooth and stays together. Refrigerate for 2 hours. If necessary, add more powdered sugar to make the dough more firm.

   When the dough has chilled, preheat oven to 350° F and melt the butter and chocolate over low heat. Stir in the hazelnuts, ¼ cup powdered sugar, and vanilla. Let cool. Roll out the dough and cut it into 3x3-inch squares. Place a heaping teaspoon of filling in the middle of each square. Roll up the filled squares and place seam side down on a greased cookie sheet. Bake for 7 minutes.

   While the cookies are cooling, make the frosting. Stir the ½ cup powdered sugar and lemon juice together until well blended. Drizzle over the cooled cookies. Makes 36 cookies.

Hazelnut Cheesecake

CRUST
1 ½ cups crushed graham crackers
1 cup hazelnuts, ground fine
6 teaspoons butter

BATTER
16 ounces cream cheese
¾ cup sugar
1 cup sour cream
3 eggs
½ cup amaretto
1 cup hazelnuts, ground fine
3 tablespoons cornstarch
6 ounces white chocolate, melted

STRAWBERRY SAUCE
1 pint strawberries
4 tablespoons sugar
2 tablespoons water

TOPPING
½ pint whipping cream
3 tablespoons sugar

Preheat oven to 350° F. Grease a 9-inch springform pan. Mix the crushed graham crackers with 1 cup finely ground hazelnuts. Melt the butter and stir it all together. Form the crust into a ball and then press it into the springform.

Beat the cream cheese, ¾ cup sugar, and sour cream together until smooth. Beat in the eggs, one at a time. Add the amaretto, 1 cup ground hazelnuts, and cornstarch. Pour in the melted chocolate and beat until all ingredients are well mixed.

Pour the batter into the pie crust and place the pan in a larger cake or roasting pan. Fill the outside pan with water. Bake in the oven for 1 hour and 15 minutes. Remove from the oven and let the cake cool.

Pick out a few perfect strawberries for decoration. Hull the remaining strawberries and cut them in half. In a saucepan, mix the strawberries with 4 tablespoons sugar and 2 tablespoons water, then boil for 10 minutes. (Serve this sauce hot or cold.)

Before serving, beat the whipping cream and 3 tablespoons of sugar together until stiff. Cover the top of the cake with the whipped cream and decorate with the reserved strawberries. Place 3 tablespoons of strawberry sauce on each plate and arrange a slice of cake in the middle of the plate. Serves 10.

Hazelnut Chocolate Bars

1 ½ sticks butter
1 cup sugar
¼ cup milk
1 ½ teaspoons vanilla
3 eggs
1 cup flour
1 teaspoon baking soda
3 tablespoons cocoa powder
½ cup sesame seeds
1 cup hazelnuts, chopped
6 ounces semi-sweet chocolate

Preheat oven to 350° F. In a saucepan, melt the butter with the sugar, then stir in the milk and vanilla. Beat in the eggs one at a time, then mix in the flour, baking soda, and cocoa powder; blend well. Add the remaining ingredients and blend, then pour the batter into a 9-inch greased and floured square or rectangular pan. Bake for 45 minutes or until a fork comes out clean. Cool before you cut into squares. Makes 35 bars.

Hazelnut Cookies

2 cups flour
¾ cup sugar
Finely grated rind of 1 lemon
2 ½ cups hazelnuts, ground
1 egg
1 ½ sticks butter
48 whole hazelnuts for decoration
1 egg white

In a large bowl, blend the flour, sugar, grated lemon rind, and ground hazelnuts. Stir in the egg. Cut the butter into small cubes, then work the cubes quickly into the flour mix. Cover and put the dough in the refrigerator for 1 ½ hours.

After 1 ½ hours, preheat the oven to 350° F. Roll the dough out on a lightly floured surface to a ¼-inch thickness. Cut the cookies out with a cookie cutter. Place a nut on each cookie. Place the cookies on a greased cookie sheet and brush with egg white. Bake for approximately 10 minutes or until very light brown. Makes 4 dozen cookies.

Hazelnut Dessert Cakes

CAKE
8 egg yolks
2 cups powdered sugar
1 ½ cups dried bread crumbs
½ cup flour
Grated rinds of 2 oranges
4 tablespoons orange juice
1 ½ cups hazelnuts, ground
8 egg whites

TOPPING
½ pint whipping cream
2 tablespoons butter
1 cup hazelnuts, ground
2 tablespoons orange liqueur
2 tablespoons sugar

Preheat oven to 350° F. Beat the egg yolks and powdered sugar together until light. Add the bread crumbs, flour, grated orange rind, orange juice, and 1 ½ cups ground nuts. In a separate bowl, beat the egg whites until stiff. Gently fold the egg whites into the other mixture. Pour this batter into greased muffin tins or a 9-inch cake pan and bake for 15 minutes or until a fork comes out clean.

To make the topping, whip the cream until stiff. In a saucepan, melt the butter and stir in all other ingredients. Continue stirring for 10 minutes or until nuts are light brown. Spread the hot nut mixture onto a greased sheet of aluminum foil. When cool, place the nut mixture on a cutting board and use a rolling pin to break it into little pieces. Stir the pieces into the whipped cream. Decorate the cakes when they have completely cooled. Makes 18 small cakes or 1 9-inch cake.

Rice and Hazelnut Dessert with Cherry Sauce

CAKE
2 ¾ cups milk
1 cup short-grained rice
4 tablespoons sugar
4 eggs
1 cup hazelnuts, chopped fine
1 teaspoon almond extract
8 tablespoons butter, melted

CHERRY SAUCE
4 cups pitted cherries
1 cup sugar
2 teaspoons cornstarch
1 cup water

In a saucepan, combine the milk, rice, and 4 tablespoons sugar; bring the mixture to a slow boil. Simmer for 15 minutes or until the rice is tender, then cool.

Preheat oven to 350° F. Separate the eggs, then beat the egg yolks into the rice mixture. Add the hazelnuts, almond extract, and butter and beat until well blended. In a separate bowl, beat the egg whites until stiff and carefully fold them into the rice mixture. Pour the batter into a greased and floured ring form. Bake for 1 hour.

In a saucepan, combine the cherries and sugar. In a cup, stir the cornstarch with the water, then pour this into the cherries and sugar. Bring to boil, then simmer for 10 minutes. Serve with the cake. The cake may be served hot or cold. Serves 6.

Hazelnut Truffle Chocolate Cake

This recipe is time consuming, but each step is fairly easy and the result is stunning. For the chocolate leaves, use rose leaves or other nontoxic houseplant leaves—they should be fairly thick.

CAKE
1 ½ sticks butter
3 cups sugar
1 cup water
6 ounces unsweetened chocolate
4 teaspoons vanilla
3 eggs
1 ½ cups sour cream
3 cups flour
3 teaspoons baking powder

FILLINGS
½ cup milk
1 stick butter
12 ounces semi-sweet chocolate
1 cup powdered sugar
4 tablespoons rum extract
3 egg yolks
1 ½ cups hazelnuts,
   chopped and toasted
½ pint whipping cream
4 tablespoons sugar

TOPPINGS
16 ounces marzipan
2 tablespoons sweet chocolate

Preheat the oven to 350° F. In a saucepan, melt the butter and stir in the sugar, water, chocolate, and vanilla. Remove from heat and let cool. Add the eggs and sour cream, then the flour and baking powder. Stir until completely smooth. Pour the batter into a 9-inch greased and floured baking pan. Bake for 40 minutes or until a fork inserted into the middle comes out clean.

In a saucepan, combine the milk, butter, chocolate, powdered sugar, and rum extract to make the truffle filling. Stir until melted and of smooth consistency, then beat in the egg yolks, one at a time. Continue stirring for 3 minutes, then remove the filling from the heat. Stir in the hazelnuts. Pour the filling into a foil-lined baking pan, cover, and place in the refrigerator for 2 hours or more.

Carefully, cut the cake into three thin layers. Place one layer on a cake plate and arrange the truffle filling on that layer. Place the second layer on top of the truffle filling. Beat the whipping cream and sugar together until stiff. Spread half of the whipped cream on this layer, then place the last layer on top.

Dust a rolling pin and a flat surface with a little powdered sugar to prevent sticking and roll out the marzipan into a flat disc. Carefully lift the marzipan off the rolling surface and place on top of the cake. Use the remaining whipped cream to decorate. Refrigerate the cake if it will be a while before serving.

Just before serving, make the chocolate leaves. In a double boiler, melt the sweet chocolate. Use a pastry brush to brush the undersides of stiff, waxy leaves with a layer of chocolate. Place in the freezer for ½ hour, then carefully peel the chocolate off of each coated leaf. Use the chocolate leaves to finish decorating the cake. Serves 16.

Peanuts

Peanuts are known as ground nuts or goobers. As the plant grows, new pods form above the ground, then grow downward and develop underground. Native to South America, the peanut was taken to West Africa by Portuguese traders during the sixth century. The nut spread to the Dutch East Indies, India, and China. The peanut was also grown by Indians more than 1,000 years ago.

Peanut oil is used for frying and sautéing and for making margarine. Low-grade peanut oil is used in soaps, face powder, shaving cream, shampoos, and paint. Peanut oil is also used to make nitroglycerin, which is used in explosives.

Peanuts are high in protein, fat, vitamin B, calcium, and iron.

No-Bake Peanut and Honey Snacks

2 cups chunky peanut butter
1 cup brown sugar
1 ¼ cups honey
1 cup peanuts, roughly chopped
¾ cup chocolate chips
3 cups cornflakes
½ cup chopped dried apricots

In a saucepan, combine the peanut butter, brown sugar, and honey. Simmer for 10 minutes over low heat, stirring continuously. Remove from heat. Add all other ingredients to the saucepan and stir until everything is well coated. Pour the mixture into a large, lightly greased baking pan. Cool for 30 minutes and cut into squares. Makes 50 snacks.

Blueberry Pecan Cake

CAKE
¾ cup sugar
½ cup butter
3 eggs
I cup sour cream
I teaspoon grated orange peel
2 cups flour
I cup pecans, ground
2 teaspoons baking powder
I teaspoon baking soda

TOPPING
I pint whipping cream
4 tablespoons sugar
3 cups blueberries, fresh or canned

Preheat oven to 375° F. Beat the sugar and butter together until fluffy; add the eggs and sour cream and mix well. Add the grated orange peel, flour, pecans, baking powder, and baking soda and blend well. Pour the batter into a 9-inch greased and floured baking pan. Bake for 45 minutes or until the cake comes away from the sides. Let it cool before removing it from the baking pan.

To make the topping, beat the whipping cream and sugar until stiff. Cut the cake in two layers. Saving ½ cup of blueberries for decoration, spread the remaining blueberries over the bottom layer of the cake. Spread half of the whipped cream over the blueberries. Place the other layer of the cake on top and decorate with the blueberries and remaining whipped cream.

Pecan Cherry Cookies

I cup butter
¾ cup sugar
2 teaspoons vanilla
2 egg yolks
2 cups flour
½ teaspoon baking powder
2 egg whites
I ½ cups pecans, chopped fine
6-ounce jar maraschino cherries

Preheat oven to 350° F. Beat the butter and sugar together until light and fluffy. Add the vanilla and the egg yolks and blend. Stir in the flour and baking powder until all is well blended. Form this dough into a long roll, then divide into approximately 30 pieces. Roll each piece into a ball and dip each ball into the egg whites and roll in the chopped pecans. Press a cherry into the middle of each cookie.

Place cookies, spaced slightly apart, on a greased cookie sheet and bake for 15 minutes. Makes 30 cookies.

Pecan Cranberry Cake

CAKE
2 cups cranberries
½ cup water
2 cups sugar
¾ cup butter
1 cup plain yogurt
3 eggs
3 cups flour
2 teaspoons baking powder
1 teaspoon baking soda
3 tablespoons orange juice
3 teaspoons grated orange peel
1 cup pecans

FROSTING
3 cups powdered sugar
¼ cup orange juice

Preheat oven to 350° F. In a saucepan, cook the cranberries in the water with ½ cup of the sugar for 10 minutes. Beat the butter and remaining 1 ½ cups sugar together until light and fluffy. Add the yogurt and eggs; beat some more. Add the flour, baking powder, baking soda, orange juice, orange peel, and pecans. Pour half of this batter into a greased and floured 9x12-inch baking pan. Spread the cranberry mixture from the saucepan over that, then pour the rest of the batter on top. Bake for 45 minutes. Remove from oven and let cool.

Mix frosting ingredients together until smooth. After the cake has cooled, spread the frosting over it. Serves 12–16.

Pecan Pie

CRUST
1 ¾ cups flour
½ cup butter or
   vegetable shortening
1 egg

FILLING
¼ pound butter
4 tablespoons cocoa powder
½ cup honey
½ cup light corn syrup
2 teaspoons vanilla
¼ teaspoon salt
4 eggs
2 cups pecan halves

TOPPING
½ pint whipping cream
2 tablespoons sugar

Knead all crust ingredients together to form a dough. Add a little cold water if the dough is too dry and crumbly. Using a rolling pin, roll the dough out. Line a greased 9-inch pie pan with the rolled-out dough.

Preheat oven to 350° F. Melt the ¼ pound of butter and blend with the cocoa powder, honey, corn syrup, vanilla, and salt until smooth. Add the eggs, one at a time, and beat until well blended. Add the pecan halves and stir. Pour the filling into the pie crust. Bake for 50 minutes.

Whip the cream and sugar together until stiff peaks are formed. Top the pie with whipped cream.

Pecan Tops

1 cup butter
¼ cup sugar
1 teaspoon baking soda
1 egg
2 teaspoons vanilla
2 ½ cups pecans, chopped fine
½ cup dates, chopped fine
2 cups flour
1 cup honey

Preheat oven to 350° F. Beat the butter and sugar until light and fluffy. Add the baking soda, eggs, and vanilla, then beat some more. Stir in the pecans, dates, and flour, then mix well. Roll this dough into small tops, then place on a greased cookie sheet. Warm the honey and, using a teaspoon, drip a little on each top. Bake for 10–15 minutes. Remove to waxed paper and let cool. Makes 70 tops.

Yellow Pecan Zucchini Cake

CAKE
2 sticks butter or margarine
2 cups sugar
4 eggs
1 cup sour cream
3 cups flour
½ cup wheat germ
3 teaspoons baking powder
1 ½ teaspoons cinnamon
½ teaspoon ginger
½ teaspoon nutmeg
2 teaspoons grated orange rind
1 cup pecans, chopped
1 cup raisins
3 cups grated yellow zucchini,
   the juice squeezed out

FROSTING
4 ounces cream cheese
2 tablespoons butter
1 cup powdered sugar
1 teaspoon vanilla
1 tablespoon lemon juice
½ cup pecans, chopped

Preheat oven to 350° F. Beat the butter with the sugar for 3 minutes, then beat in the eggs and sour cream. Add the flour, wheat germ, baking powder, spices, and orange rind and blend well. Stir in the pecans, raisins, and zucchini. Pour the batter into a greased and floured 9-inch baking pan and bake for 1 hour and 15 minutes. Let cool.

While the cake cools, make the frosting. Beat the cream cheese and butter together. Add the powdered sugar and beat until smooth. Blend in the vanilla and lemon juice. Spread the frosting over the top and sides of cooled cake. Sprinkle with pecans.

Plantation Pecan Cake

1 ½ cups sugar
3 eggs
1 ½ cups sifted flour
1 teaspoon baking powder
½ teaspoon salt
1 ½ cups pecans, chopped fine
1 teaspoon vanilla
½ cup butter
½ cup milk
Powdered sugar

Preheat oven to 375° F. Beat the sugar and eggs until stiff. Blend in all dry ingredients including the nuts. Melt the vanilla, butter and milk in a saucepan and cool. Beat all ingredients together. Pour the batter into a 9-inch cake pan and bake for 30 minutes. When the cake is completely cool, carefully remove it from the pan. Dust the cake with dry powdered sugar. Serves 12.

Piñon Nut Cookies

⅔ cup butter, at room temperature
½ cup brown sugar
2 egg yolks
¾ teaspoon vanilla
2 cups flour
¼ teaspoon nutmeg
1 ½ tablespoons grated orange rind
2 tablespoons honey
¾ cup piñon nuts, chopped

In a large bowl, beat the butter and brown sugar until fluffy. Add the egg yolks and vanilla and beat more. Sift in the flour and nutmeg, blend well and add the grated orange rind. Refrigerate the dough for 1 ½ hours.

Preheat oven to 350° F. Roll the dough out and cut into 4-inch long crescents. Place crescents on a greased cookie sheet. Warm the honey slightly and brush each cookie with it. Sprinkle the pine nuts on top and bake for approximately 10 minutes. Let the cookies cool on the cookie sheet before serving. Makes 2 dozen cookies.

Pistachio Chocolate Truffles

To vary this recipe, add nuts to the chocolate truffles, and roll them in chocolate sprinkles. You can also add ½ – ¾ cup fine cookie crumbs to the truffles to increase the yield.

1 ¼ cups whipping cream
16 ounces semi-sweet chocolate, chopped
½ cup butter
2 teaspoons rum extract
1 cup powdered sugar
1 cup pistachios, chopped into small pieces

In a heavy-bottomed pot, combine the cream, chocolate, butter, and rum extract. Over low heat, stir until melted and smooth. Gradually beat in the powdered sugar. Cover the pan and chill in the refrigerator for 1 hour.

With a teaspoon, scoop up the chocolate mixture and, using your hands, form into small balls. Roll each ball in the nuts; store in an airtight container in a cool place. Makes 32 truffles.

Pistachio Ice Cream

6 egg yolks
1 cup sugar
2 cups heavy cream
1 cup pistachios, chopped
Green food coloring
2 teaspoons almond extract

Combine the egg yolks and sugar and beat until stiff. In a saucepan, heat 1 cup of cream. Quickly stir the egg mixture into the hot cream. Add the almond extract. Continue stirring until it becomes a thick sauce. Remove from heat, then let cool. Beat the rest of the cream until stiff, then fold into the egg sauce. Chill this mixture in the freezer for one hour, then beat it until fluffy. Stir in the pistachios and green food coloring. Pour into a mold, cover, and freeze overnight. Remove the ice cream from the freezer 20 minutes before serving. Decorate with sprigs of mint or slices of kiwi. Serves 6.

The leftover egg whites can be used to make Danish almond macaroons (see recipe page 73), which require 5 egg whites.

Greek Walnut Cake

CAKE

1 ½ sticks butter
1 cup powdered sugar
5 eggs
1 ½ cups flour
2 teaspoons baking powder
1 teaspoon cinnamon
¼ teaspoon ground cloves
6 tablespoons brandy
4 cups walnuts, chopped

SYRUP

2 tablespoons grated orange peel
1 cup sugar
1 cup water
4 whole cloves
1 cinnamon stick, or ½ teaspoon
   ground cinnamon
3 tablespoons brandy

Preheat oven to 350° F. Beat the butter and powdered sugar together until light and fluffy. Separate the egg yolks from the egg whites. Beat the yolks into the butter mixture. Add the flour, baking powder, cinnamon, and ground cloves; mix well. Stir in the 6 tablespoons brandy and walnuts. Pour the batter into a greased 9-inch pan and bake for 45 minutes. Let cool.

   In a saucepan, combine all syrup ingredients except the 3 tablespoons brandy. Simmer over low heat for 15 minutes. Remove the cinnamon sticks and cloves; stir in the brandy.

   After the cake has cooled, cut it into squares. Pour the syrup over the cake squares. Cool the squares overnight before serving to allow the flavors to blend together. Serves 12.

Orange Walnut Cookies

½ cup butter
¾ cup sugar
Grated rind and juice of 1 orange
1 egg
2 cups flour
½ teaspoon cinnamon
¼ teaspoon cardamom
½ cup walnuts, ground
10 ounces semi-sweet chocolate

Beat the butter, sugar, orange rind, and egg until fluffy. Blend in all other ingredients (including orange juice) except the chocolate. Cool dough in the refrigerator for 3 hours or overnight.

   Preheat oven to 400° F. With a rolling pin, roll out the dough. Using a round or other-shaped cookie cutter, cut cookies out of the dough. Place the cookies on a greased cookie sheet and bake for 8 minutes. When the cookies have cooled, melt the chocolate in a small saucepan. Dip the edges of each cookie in the melted chocolate. Makes 30 cookies.

Walnut and Pistachio Baklava

PASTRY
1 pound fresh phyllo dough
2 ½ sticks butter

NUT FILLING
3 cups walnuts, chopped fine
2 cups pistachio nuts, chopped fine
1 cup fine dry bread crumbs
2 teaspoons cinnamon

SYRUP
3 cups sugar
1 ½ cups water
1 cup honey
4 cloves
6 tablespoons brandy

Cover the phyllo dough with a damp towel. Melt the butter and set aside. Grease an 11x15-inch baking pan. Combine all nut filling ingredients.

Place 10 layers of phyllo dough in the baking pan, brushing each layer with the melted butter. Spread a thin layer of the nut filling on top of the layered dough, then layer 3 more sheets of phyllo dough on top of the filling, brushing each new layer with butter. Repeat this process until you have used all of the nut filling. Finish the process with 12 more sheets of phyllo dough, continuing to brush each layer with butter.

Preheat oven to 350°F. With a knife, cut the baklava into diamonds. Press one whole clove into the middle of each diamond. Bake the baklava for 40 minutes or until it is golden brown.

While the baklava is baking, prepare the syrup. Combine all syrup ingredients and simmer over low heat for about 15 minutes. Remove the baklava from the oven and remove the cloves. Let cool slightly. Pour the syrup over the warm baklava. Let the baklava sit for a couple hours or overnight before serving. Makes 40 baklava.

Apples with Walnut Stuffing and Vanilla Cream Sauce

APPLES AND STUFFING
4 large apples
4 tablespoons butter
4 tablespoons brown sugar
1 teaspoon cinnamon
½ cup walnuts, chopped
1 cup white wine

VANILLA CREAM SAUCE
4 egg yolks
3 tablespoons sugar
2 cups milk
1 ½ teaspoons vanilla

Preheat oven to 350° F. Cut the top off of each apple. Core the apples and, with a spoon, hollow each apple out a bit. Set aside the apple meat. In a bowl, beat the butter, brown sugar, and cinnamon until light and fluffy. Stir in the nuts and apple meat. Fill the apples with this mixture and place them in a small baking pan. Pour the wine over the apples and bake for 45 minutes, basting occasionally.

While the apples bake, beat the egg yolks and sugar together with an electric beater until thickened. Beat in the milk and vanilla. Pour the mixture into a thick-bottomed saucepan and stir over low heat until it boils. Let cool.

Pour the cream sauce over the hot apples and serve. Serves 4.

Walnut Chocolate Chip Pie

CRUST
2 cups chocolate cake or cookie crumbs
1 cup crumbled graham crackers
1 egg
1 stick butter

FILLING
1 stick butter
¾ cup sugar
2 eggs
2 teaspoons vanilla
1 cup flour
6 ounces or 1 cup semi-sweet
    chocolate chips
1 cup walnuts, chopped

TOPPING
½ pint whipping cream
2 tablespoons sugar

Combine the cake or cookie crumbs and the graham cracker crumbs. Beat in the egg, then knead in 1 stick of butter. Form the dough into a ball and place it in a 9-inch greased pie pan. Using your fingers, press the dough out to cover the inside of the pan.

Preheat oven to 350° F. Beat the second stick of butter and ¾ cup sugar together until light. Add the 2 eggs, vanilla, and flour. Blend well, then add the chocolate chips and walnuts. Pour this into the pie shell and bake for 40 minutes. Let the pie cool.

Meanwhile, whip the cream and 2 tablespoons sugar together until stiff peaks are formed. Top the cooled pie with the whipped cream. (Ice cream also makes a nice topping.) Serves 8.

Walnut Carrot Cake

CAKE
1 ⅓ cups butter, at room temperature
1 ½ cups sugar
1 ½ teaspoons vanilla
4 eggs
2 cups flour
2 teaspoons baking powder
1 teaspoon cinnamon
½ teaspoon ground nutmeg
½ teaspoon ground cloves
3 cups grated carrots
1 ½ cups walnuts, chopped

LEMON CREAM CHEESE FROSTING
¼ cup butter, at room temperature
6 ounces cream cheese, at
   room temperature
4 teaspoons freshly squeezed lemon juice
2 cups powdered sugar

DECORATION
½ cup walnuts, chopped
12 walnut halves

Preheat oven to 350 ° F. In a large bowl, beat the 1 ⅓ cups butter, sugar, and vanilla for 10 minutes with an electric beater. Add the eggs, one at a time, and beat well. Add the flour, baking powder, and spices and beat until well blended. Stir in the carrots and walnuts. Pour the batter into a 9x13-inch greased and floured baking pan. Bake for 55 minutes or until a fork inserted in the cake comes out clean. Let the cake cool in the pan before removing.

While the cake cools, beat the ¼ cup butter and cream cheese until smooth. Stir in the lemon juice and powdered sugar. Beat for 5 minutes. Spread the frosting on top of the cake and decorate with the chopped walnuts and walnut halves. Serves 12.

Walnut Mocha Cheesecake

This cake is not too sweet, rich in flavor and easy to make.

2 cups chocolate cookies, crushed
16 ounces cream cheese
1 cup sour cream
2 cups walnuts, ground fine
3 teaspoons cornstarch
3 eggs
12 ounces semi-sweet chocolate, melted
3 tablespoons Grand Marnier or coffee

Press the cookie crumbs into the bottom of a 9-inch springform pan.

Preheat oven to 350° F. Beat the cream cheese and sour cream together until smooth. Add the ground walnuts and cornstarch, and beat until batter is smooth. Add the eggs one at a time. Melt the chocolate with the Grand Marnier or coffee and stir this into the rest of the batter. Pour the batter on top of the cookie crumbs and place the springform inside a larger pan containing water. Bake for 1 hour. Tastes great with whipped cream. Serves 8.

Shown opposite:
Walnut Carrot Cake.

Banana Cake with Walnuts

BATTER

1 ¼ cups sugar
1 ½ sticks butter, at room temperature
2 teaspoons vanilla
3 eggs
1 cup walnuts, ground fine
2 ½ cups flour
2 teaspoons baking powder
1 teaspoon ginger
2 teaspoons cinnamon
5 bananas
¼ cup strong coffee, cold

FROSTING

1 cup powdered sugar
3 ounces sweet or semi-sweet chocolate
2 teaspoons water

Preheat oven to 350° F. In a large bowl, beat the sugar, butter, and vanilla with an electric beater for 10 minutes. Add the eggs, one at a time. Mix the walnuts, flour, baking powder, and spices and add to the batter. Stir until all ingredients are well blended. Mash the bananas with a fork and add them and the coffee to the batter. Stir well. Pour the batter into a 9-inch springform pan or equivalent. Bake in the oven for 40 minutes or until a fork comes out clean. Let the cake cool before you remove it from the form.

Pour all the frosting ingredients into a double boiler and stir over medium heat until the butter and chocolate have melted, then spread over the cake. You can decorate with banana slices dipped in some of the chocolate sauce or in lemon juice if you are going to eat it right away. Serves 12.

Shown opposite: Banana Cake with Walnuts.

Index

About the Author

Christin Fjeld Drake grew up in Oslo, Norway, where as a child she ate as little as her mother would let her get away with. She first started to appreciate food when she was sixteen, when she and her first love, Ørnolf, worked together in a delicatessen after school. Later, as a student in a Catholic nursing school, the nuns prepared scrumptious treats for the students who lived in the residence halls, and Christin delighted the sisters by taking an interest in learning how to prepare their favorite recipes. Christin's cooking skills were rounded out during her travels through Europe, her time working at a British private school in the very international city of Athens, and her stint as a restaurateur in Flagstaff, Arizona, where she now lives with her husband, Steve, and her children, Kjersti, Thor, and Bjørn.